# Thinking about fostering?

## The definitive guide to fostering in the UK

**Henrietta Bond**

coramBAAF
ADOPTION & FOSTERING ACADEMY

Published by
CoramBAAF Adoption and Fostering Academy
41 Brunswick Square
London WC1N 1AZ
www.corambaaf.org.uk

Coram Academy Limited, registered as a company limited by guarantee in England
and Wales number 9697712, part of the Coram group, charity number 312278

British Library Cataloguing in Publication Data
A catalogue record for this book is available from the British Library

ISBN 978 1 910039 54 0

Project management by Jo Francis, Publications, CoramBAAF
Designed by Helen Joubert Designs
Typeset by Fravashi Aga
Printed in Great Britain by TJ International

Trade distribution by Turnaround Publisher Services, Unit 3, Olympia Trading Estate,
Coburg Road, London N22 6TZ

# Contents

## Acknowledgements

At CoramBAAF, thanks to my editor, Jo Francis, and also Paul Adams, Jacqui Lawrence and Katrina Wilson for their help.

I would also like to thank the many foster carers, care-experienced young people and adults, and the social workers who have given me so many helpful insights over the years. I'd particularly like to thank (in no particular order) Matt Langsford, Peter and Leah and Theresa Green. Also thanks to Angela Sitoe from Sefton, Jackie Sanders (Fostering Network), Steve Stockley (Fosterline) and Harvey Gallagher (Nationwide Association of Fostering Providers). Thanks also to Fiona Darlington-Black and Anna McGorry for reading and commenting on an early version of the book.

## Note about the author

Henrietta Bond is a writer, coach and communications consultant who has worked in the field of adoption, fostering and leaving care for nearly 30 years. Previously BAAF's media and information officer, she became a freelance consultant and journalist, and worked on a variety of projects, including group work with care-experienced children and young people. She has written a number of guides and her trilogy of novels for teenagers, the Control Freak series (available from CoramBAAF), came out of her close work with children and young people.

Henrietta is passionate about giving children and young people a voice and helping them to develop resilience and self-esteem, and is keen to develop the potential of coaching to help young people have more control over their own lives. As a writer, she also helps young people find creative ways to express themselves. Henrietta recognises that she has as much to learn from young people as they have to learn from her.

# Introduction

You don't have to look far to find mentions of fostering in the media these days. Whether you're watching a TV soap opera, visiting a library, or picking up the latest copy of a magazine, stories about fostering are everywhere. Sometimes it's heart-rending newspaper articles on carers who've given "loving homes" to hundreds of children, or memoirs of children "rescued" from years of appalling neglect and abuse. Sometimes it's accounts of "wicked" foster carers imprisoned for abusing their roles, alarming documentaries about the behavioural problems of looked after children, or the celebrity who made good despite a childhood in care. However it's represented, fostering is usually the subject of extreme drama of one kind or another – all very well as something to read or listen to when you're putting your feet up with a cup of coffee, but quite different when you're considering becoming a foster carer.

This book sets out to cut through the dramatic hype, and give you an honest, straightforward and helpful insight into what it really means to look after other people's children in your own home. It doesn't pull any punches about the reality of fostering. Fostering is challenging, and requires considerable amounts of commitment, stickability, perseverance and open-mindedness – to name but a

few of the qualities required. Having an anxious, volatile or
seriously withdrawn child or young person under your roof 24
hours a day, seven days a week, is not something you enter into
lightly. But if watching this child develop confidence, walk away
from situations where once they'd have exploded, or join in at
family mealtimes, knowing that you've helped them to achieve
this, is something you'd find motivating and rewarding – then
fostering could be for you.

It's not possible to be exact about the number of children fostered in
any year because children may enter and leave foster care several
times over a year, but as a snapshot, Government figures show that
on the night of 31 March 2015, there were around 64,000 children
in foster placements across the UK.

Children and young people come into the "care system" for a
number of reasons. This may relate to problems in their own family,
such as illnesses – including life-threatening conditions, or severe
mental health issues – or because of an addiction that their parents
have developed, sometimes in response to their own difficult
childhoods. Many children will have experienced neglect or abuse by
a member of their family or somebody living in the household. For
some young people, it's a breakdown of communication in their
family that leads to unmanageable relationships, or the young
person may have their own history of drugs, alcohol or offending
behaviour. Some young people will be unaccompanied asylum-
seekers fleeing violence in their homelands and may have
experienced considerable trauma in the process.

Some older young people may prefer to live in residential settings
because they are fed up with family life, but for most children a
foster family will provide them with the best type of temporary or
long-term care.

Whatever the reason a child or young person needs foster care, it
probably won't be an easy process for them. However much a child
has experienced disruption, mistreatment or neglect, they will still

find it hard to adjust to a new environment, especially if it is very different to their own. Things that are commonplace in some families – like eating meals together or going to bed at a certain time – may be strange to a child who has lived in a chaotic household. Even if a child is relieved to be away from abuse or mistreatment, they are likely to worry about their brothers and sisters, or a parent who is still living with an abusive partner.

As a foster carer, you will need lots of patience and empathy for children coming into your home. You will need to be prepared to be flexible, take things slowly and make adjustments for children who are angry, frightened or bewildered. You may find yourself coping with types of behaviour and situations you have little or no previous experience of handling – and will understand why fostering services require prospective carers to have careful assessment, preparation and training.

You will be expected to have contact with a child's own birth family – usually in a specialist contact centre but maybe in a community setting. Again, you will receive training and preparation for this, but new carers often find it hard to imagine. Certainly you may find it difficult to interact comfortably with people you know to have harmed or neglected their child, and you may find yourself questioning why these meetings are necessary. However, you may also find it surprisingly helpful to discover that the child's family are "normal people" who, for all sorts of complex reasons, are unable to care for or protect their child, and are not the "monsters" you'd let yourself imagine.

You may also be surprised to discover the emphasis on the "professionalisation" of foster care. Today, foster carers are expected to be part of the "fostering team" and to demonstrate that they can meet a range of standards, set out in legislation. You will be asked to work towards goals established with the child's social worker and behave at all times as a "professional". You will be expected to keep notes and write reports, and you may even be asked to go to court to give your experience of looking after a particular child. You will receive financial recompense so you are not out of pocket, and, in some cases, a fee for your work. At the same time, you will also be required to be a kind, supportive, warm and approachable parent-like figure for the child; someone they can relate to, and who they believe genuinely cares about them and is ready to fight their corner when they need this.

Choosing to foster is a life-changing decision and should not be taken lightly. The children you foster will always be a part of your family, whether in memory or in person. This book will try to answer as many of your questions as possible so you can think through whether this is something you want to do. It will also give you lots of pointers about getting the best out of the experience – enabling you to think about what you need to know if you decide to start the process.

## A shortage of carers

There is always a need to recruit more foster carers, and you will hear reports in the media about shortages of carers. This doesn't always mean that children who need foster care won't be placed with a carer. But it can mean that a child is placed with the only carer who has a vacancy and is able to take them, rather than a carer who more fully matches the individual child's needs. For example, a teenager who would benefit from living with someone experienced in looking after teenagers and who lives near to the young person's school may end up staying with a foster carer living on the other side of the region, who normally specialises in fostering younger children.

For this reason, fostering services are often quite specific about the types of foster carers they need, so not every service recruits carers for all ages of children. This can sometimes make it seem that new carers aren't needed – but you may find that other services are looking for just what you have to offer.

Despite the stereotypes you often see on TV and in newspapers, there really is no "typical" foster carer. Children and young people have a wide range of needs and this means a very wide range of people are required to meet these. Some children will benefit from living in a two-parent household with other children, but some may need the one-to-one attention of being the only child in the household, and may prefer living with only one adult. Fostering services welcome people who are single, married, divorced, cohabiting, gay or lesbian – as long as they are able to meet children's needs. Carers don't have to have their own children but they do need experience and understanding of caring for children, which might vary from babysitting for nephews and nieces to working as a teacher, social worker or sports coach.

What most foster carers have in common is that they are highly motivated – although they may be motivated in many different ways. Research (Fostering Network, 2013) identifies three different "drivers" that motivate people to foster.

- Some people foster because they are very family- and home-focused and have a strong need to "do the right thing".
- Some people are very success-oriented and enjoy the challenge of doing a great job on behalf of the children they care for.
- Some people are highly motivated by a sense of social justice and want to make a difference in society.

You probably won't be conscious of exactly why you are drawn to fostering and if you ask existing carers about their motivation, they will give a range of answers. Some will tell you they chose it because they enjoyed bringing up their own family and felt they still had lots to offer; some will feel they have a wealth of professional or personal experience and wanted to make good use of it; and some will say that they simply love having children in their lives. But when you ask foster carers what motivates them to continue through the times when the going gets tough, they'll tell you that it's the reward of knowing they have made a difference to the future of a child or young person.

## Fostering today

> So what is my exact role? Am I an employee? A mum? A
> carer? I like to think of myself as a professional parent!
> *Rosamond, foster carer, quoted in 'Who am I and what*
> *do I do?'*

In the past, fostering was often seen as a way of putting a roof
over a child's head, and it was felt that giving the child love was all
that was needed. But today it's recognised that the important role
of foster carers is to help children cope with difficult and painful
experiences, regain lost confidence and prepare for the future.
Therefore fostering services expect carers to work closely with social
workers and other professionals, to carry out an agreed plan for each
child. Some foster carers choose to foster as a career choice, whilst
others see themselves more as substitute parents, but all carers
receive payment to cover the costs of having a child in their home.

Fostering services don't expect applicants to come with all the
skills and knowledge needed. If they believe someone has the
commitment, enthusiasm and child-centred attitude they are looking
for, they offer preparation and training. All foster carers then have
to be approved in order to care for other people's children. Once
they become foster carers, they receive ongoing training and
support to continue to develop these skills.

This guide covers issues such as:

- how people become foster carers;
- what children might feel about coming into care;
- how to settle a child into your home;
- the law and regulations; and
- working as part of the team around the child.

Many of these issues are illustrated by the experiences of real foster
carers, who speak openly about the things they've found difficult or
challenging, as well as the rewards and high points. There are also

quotes from young people who speak about their experiences of being in foster care and what they need from carers.

We're sure that from reading these quotes, you will realise that fostering can make a real difference to the lives of unhappy, confused and anxious children and young people. But restoring a child's faith in themselves and the world around them doesn't happen overnight, and is a demanding task that requires perseverance, patience and the ability to always keep the child's best interests at the heart of everything you do. We hope this book will help you make an informed decision about whether this is something that you and your family (if you have one) are ready to consider.

> **Because it was a very friendly, homely environment, I just picked up on it so well that I just sort of let myself go…I just became happy I suppose.**
> *24-year-old formerly fostered adult, quoted in 'Part of the Family'*

## Note to this edition

The contents of this book apply to England, Wales and Scotland. Although Northern Ireland is not specifically covered, many of the practices and issues are the same (although in Northern Ireland children are in the care of Health and Social Services Trusts, not local authorities). Some of the legislation varies slightly between the four nations, and for the sake of simplicity, only major differences are highlighted here.

Local authorities place children for fostering either with their own "in-house" foster carers, or with carers approved and supported by independent fostering providers (IFPs); these may be commercial services or not-for-profit organisations such as charities. All of these services are inspected by Ofsted to comply with fostering regulations. For convenience, the term "fostering service" is used in this book to refer to both local authorities and IFPs.

---

**INDEPENDENT FOSTERING PROVIDER (IFP)**

This is the term used to describe independent services that recruit, train and support foster carers to look after children on behalf of local authorities. Local authorities approach IFPs when they do not have foster carers of their own who can meet the particular needs of a child. IFPs must meet the same standards as local authority fostering services.

---

This book does not specifically cover "family and friends" or "kinship" fostering, which is when relatives or close family friends of a child look after them and they are approved as carers by a local authority. Some aspects of family and friends care may be similar to fostering unrelated children, but other aspects may be different. For more information, see *One of the Family* by Hedi Argent (published by CoramBAAF).

This book also does not cover "private fostering", which is a private arrangement made by a child's parents with another person – who might be a friend or someone who has decided to become a private foster carer. For more information about private fostering, see CoramBAAF's Advice Note, *Private Fostering*.

The book also does not cover Fostering for Adoption or concurrency. In Fostering for Adoption, people are approved as adopters, but are then temporarily approved as foster carers for a named child – they will provide foster care for the child, and become adopters if the child cannot go home. In concurrent planning, people are similarly approved as both adopters and foster carers, by specialist schemes, fostering a child before becoming adopters if the child cannot go home. For more information on these forms of care, see *Adopting a Child* by Jenifer Lord (published by CoramBAAF).

Changes occur from time to time in legislation and practice that may affect fostering services, foster carers or the children and young people they look after. The information in this book was correct at the time of going to press (July 2016).

# 1

# Why children need fostering

> I can't imagine where my brother and I would be now without our foster carers. They've treated us like their own children – wanted good stuff for us and pushed us to make the best of ourselves – and we've both done really well as a result. Although I'm the first to admit we haven't always been easy to look after.
> *Craig, young adult, who was fostered*

Fostering is usually an arrangement designed to provide a child with family life when the child can't live with their family. Many children who are fostered return to their families, although some will stay in foster care for long periods, or may go on to other sorts of care, such as adoption.

Children of all ages – from babies through to adolescents – may need to live with foster carers for anything from a single night to several months or years.

## Why may a child need fostering?

There can be a number of reasons why a child or young person needs fostering. Their parents may be unable to look after the child because of illness or mental health problems, or they may have a drug or alcohol-related problem. The family may be additionally facing debt, housing problems or discrimination from neighbours, adding to the pressures they are already experiencing.

Some parents may be the victims of domestic violence and abuse, which can have a very adverse affect on their children. If they are unable to separate from their aggressive partner, it may be necessary for the child to be removed from the household, to protect the child's long-term emotional needs, and also perhaps to protect them from violence. The child may be very worried about leaving their parent behind in this type of situation and will need a lot of support to manage their worries about their parent or other children still living in the family.

Alternatively, it might be that someone living in the family home has seriously neglected or physically or sexually abused the child. This may not be the parent themselves but another relative, sibling, lodger or a new partner of the parent. Some parents will be very quick to seek help if they know that their child is at risk of abuse, but others may not want to face up to this shocking reality; or, because of abuse and neglect they have suffered themselves, may consider that this is just a "normal" part of life.

For parents who have had very difficult childhoods themselves or who don't have any support from family or friends, there can be a real struggle when additional pressures pile up in their lives. Sometimes a parent who was just about coping, with the support of a partner, is put under much extra pressure when a relationship ends through separation or bereavement. They may start to withdraw from their responsibilities as a parent, and be unable to prioritise their child's needs.

> My mum loves me, I know that, but she's had mental health issues for many years and often she couldn't look after herself, let alone me. In some ways I've grown up

with two families – my foster family where I live most of
the time, and my mum, who I spend time with when
she's well enough.
*Calum, young adult who grew up in foster care*

## Do disabled children need fostering?

Disabled children may need fostering because their parents are
finding it hard to cope with the child's physical or learning
disabilities. Parents may need help to be able to care for their child
properly. It may be that a disabled child has been physically hurt or
sexually abused or neglected, and needs to live with a foster carer
while plans are made for their future – just the same as any other
child in such a distressing situation.

Having a disabled child in your family can make it very difficult for
parents to make sure all their children get a "fair share" of their time
and attention, and short break care (sometimes known as respite
care) allows parents to have quality time with the other children in
the family. This can apply to foster carers as well as birth families –
and some respite carers provide support to other foster carers.

Some foster carers offer short break care. This is usually for a short
period – perhaps a weekend once a month or the occasional week –
that is agreed between the family and the fostering service. During
short breaks the child gains new experiences in a new environment,
and the parents have some time to themselves to relax and replenish
their energies.

## Do asylum-seeking children need fostering?

Asylum-seeking children and young people may also need foster
care for a variety of reasons. They may have been sent to this
country to get them away from war or the threat of serious danger
in their home country. Their parents may not be able to escape

themselves and may have paid for someone to take their child to a place of safety. Some children may arrive in this country having experienced terrible things – the death, rape or torture of relatives and friends in their homeland, followed by traumatic journeys by land and sea, and rejection by other countries. If a parent has brought them to this country, they may be ill or suffering from trauma, and unable to look after them.

Children who have lived in situations of great danger have often learnt to be very secretive about their past (for the protection of their families and themselves), and there may also be serious cultural and language barriers that foster carers will need to overcome, to help these children start to relax and begin to thrive.

> **The young sibling group I fostered were the children of a woman whose husband had "disappeared" in her home country. I guess she'd also been through awful experiences herself as she arrived here very ill from HIV. She was too exhausted to have the day-to-day care of them but still wanted to see them frequently. Sadly she died within a year of arriving. I cared for the children and prepared them for a move to an adoptive family.**
> *Asha, foster carer*

## Do all children who come into foster care have problems?

Every child is different and will react differently to the circumstances in which they find themselves. However, most children or young people who need fostering are likely to be experiencing difficulties in their lives. Some children may feel angry and confused about the things that have happened to them, and distressed about being separated from their families. Often their behaviour will reflect this. Some may express this in anger, some may become very withdrawn, and some children seem to take these things in their stride. Some will have experienced severe trauma and may need a lot of therapeutic input to help them manage their experiences.

Foster carers receive training to help them think about how to respond to children's needs and cope with challenging behaviour. They also receive support from their supervising social worker at the fostering service and can ask for advice or extra training, if they need this. If you become a foster carer, it's advisable to take up all training opportunities that come your way and to top up your skills as much as possible.

## How does a child enter foster care?

Sometimes parents will turn to their local authority for help, but it may be that the child's behaviour, lack of concentration or general appearance of neglect will alert schools or concerned neighbours that the family is in some form of crisis. Some older children will actively seek help from teachers, police or children's social services, but will often feel torn by loyalty towards their parents and other siblings.

In some cases there may be tension between young people and their parents or serious problems in the home, and a teenager feels that they need to be away from home for a while. Sometimes the young person has developed problems of their own, such as misuse of drugs or alcohol or has got caught up with friends who have led them into offending behaviour. A young person may be remanded by a court into foster care. In Scotland, they may be required to live in foster care as part of a supervision order.

In most cases, the child or young person will not be known to the foster carer. However, in some cases, a residential worker, youth worker or teacher, who has formed a close link with a child who needs foster care, might apply to a local authority fostering service to be considered for this role.

## Are children from the same family always fostered together?

For some children in troubled, neglectful or abusive families, the relationship with their brothers and sisters may be the most important and nurturing that they have. These children can really benefit from being placed with their siblings when other aspects of their family life seem to be turning upside down. So in many cases, social workers will try to find foster carers who can look after brothers and sisters together, or if this isn't possible, two carers who live near to each other so that siblings can maintain close contact.

Sometimes, however, children will benefit from living apart from their siblings. This may be when an older child has spent a lot of time trying to "parent" his or her neglected siblings and continues to worry about their welfare. He or she may find it very hard to allow the foster carer to take over responsibility for the younger children, and equally may find it hard to allow themselves to be cared for. Some time to "be a child" will be important for a child in this situation, but regular sibling contact will also be important to maintain relationships and keep the older child from worrying.

In some cases a child who has been abused – sexually or physically – may pose a physical threat to their siblings. This can be a difficult situation and social workers and the court may need to make complex decisions about what is best for the individual children.

As a foster carer, you should expect to receive enough information to understand the situation of a child you are caring for, including why a child is or is not being placed with siblings.

## How is fostering different to adoption?

Fostering is different to adoption because when a child is in foster care, the plan is usually to try and help the child return home – and most children who come into foster care do return home to their families.

But when a child is adopted, all "parental responsibility" for the child passes to the new family – as though the child had been born into that family. The child continues to be a member of the new family even when they reach adulthood – just as any other child born to that family would be.

Children will be fostered, or adopted, depending on their individual situation and what will be the best way to provide them with security and "permanence".

When you foster a child, you take care of the child on a day-to-day basis. You offer the child a caring and supportive family environment – but you will not be "replacing" the child's parents. Fostering is a bit like caring for a friend's or relative's child – you provide very high quality care, but you don't encourage the child to see you as a replacement for their parents.

> These children already have their own mums and dads, they don't need me to be their mum. Instead, I think of myself a bit like an aunt– who really cares about them and wants what is best for them.
> *Veronique, foster carer*

---

### DELEGATED AUTHORITY

While, as a foster carer, you will not have a legal responsibility for the child, you will have Delegated Authority, which gives you the right to make some decisions about important everyday things in the child's life. This may include, for example, sleepovers at a friend's house and going on school trips, so the child or young person can enjoy a life as similar to their peers as possible.

## What if the child can't go home?

When there is no possibility for a child to return home to their parents, attempts will be made to see if anyone else in the family can care for them. If this is not possible, a family must be found who can provide "permanence" for the child, to allow them to feel as secure as possible. This could be through long-term fostering or adoption.

In long-term fostering, a child stays with their foster carers until they reach adulthood. Some foster carers may obtain a legal order that makes it clear for the carers and child that the child will not be moving on.

Some foster carers may adopt children whom they have cared for, but fostering should never be considered as a route into adoption. When you approach a service, you should think carefully about whether fostering or adoption will be the best option for your family, because they are quite different.

# 2

# Different types of fostering

Originally we were approved to take under-fives but these days we take teenagers, some of them pretty challenging. How did that happen – I really don't know, but we've done a fair bit of training and gained a lot of knowledge and experience over the years, and it's kind of evolved.
*Mandy, experienced foster carer*

Foster care encompasses children with a wide range of needs and from birth up to young adulthood, so there are different types of fostering to suit different children. Some foster carers specialise in fostering particular groups of children, for example, looking after teenagers on remand, or pre-school children, but others combine several types.

The names given to different types of fostering may refer to how long the care lasts, e.g. emergency or short-term, or to things such as the age group of the children and young people, or to their particular needs.

## Types of foster care

Individual services may have slightly different ways of referring to "types" of fostering, so the information below is an outline of how the categories are normally divided. If you are unsure about the terms a fostering service is using, you can discuss this with them.

## Short-term

This is when carers look after children while plans are made for the children's future. As a foster carer, you probably won't receive a lot of initial warning about a short-term placement, but wherever possible fostering services will take care to place a child somewhere that meets as many of their needs as possible. You may also have a chance to meet the child before they are placed with you – but this may not always be possible as short-term placements are sometimes made at fairly short notice.

You will probably be required to work in a very task-oriented way with the child, as well as providing a lot of encouragement, support and reassurance. For example, the child's social worker may want you to focus on particular aspects of the child's development, such as helping him or her to build confidence, manage challenging behaviours and coping with the uncertainty of whether or not they will be returning to their family. A short-term placement can be as long as 12–18 months.

Short-term foster care also includes emergency care. This is when children or young people need somewhere safe to stay immediately for a few nights. Typically, you might get a call from your social worker asking if you can take a child, later that day, whose parent has been admitted to hospital or taken into police custody, or the child has just been removed from their home because of serious abuse or neglect. Some carers specialise in taking emergency placements, but others may agree to take one because they recognise the importance of providing a safe, caring environment for a distressed and frightened child. You will need to be very flexible and understanding when a child comes to your home in these situations. You will probably know very little about him or her, and he or she will know nothing about you, so you cannot expect the child to instantly adapt to your family life: you will need to be adaptable and flexible to their needs.

> We try and have stuff ready for when children come to us. Things like spare toothbrushes and spare pyjamas, and some day clothes as well. Some children come in just the clothes they stand up in. Sometimes they are also filthy and you're longing to get them into a bath, but you have to be a bit careful about this. You want to make the child feel as welcome as you possibly can and plunging them straight into the shower can be alarming for a child who isn't used to this. You also have to think about what they're most likely to want to eat. You might be strongly into wholemeal and organic food but you have to think about whether that child has grown up eating chicken nuggets and white bread sandwiches...and try and give them whatever will feel most natural for them in those first couple of days.
> *Karen, emergency and short-term foster carer*

## Long-term

This is when a child lives with long-term foster carers until they reach adulthood and are ready to live independently. Not all children who cannot return to their families want to be adopted, especially older children or those who continue to have regular contact with relatives. As a foster carer, you will be asked to provide "permanency" for that child, so they can settle into your family and have a sense of security and continuity. You should definitely have a chance to meet a child or young person before a long-term placement is made, and in some cases a fostering panel will need to approve the child's placement. This is to ensure that the child has been matched as appropriately as possible with carers who can best meet the child's long-term needs.

## STAYING PUT

In England, recent changes to legislation mean that local authorities have a duty to support young people to remain with their foster carers after the age of 18, and up to the age of 25, if the young person and the foster carer want this.

See *Staying Put*, published by The Children's Partnership: www.ncb.org.uk/media/1154341/staying_put.pdf

In Scotland, Staying Put guidance encourages this but at the time of publication the duties of local authorities were still under review.

In Wales, there is a requirement for local authorities to ask fostered young people and their carers if they wish to enter into a 'When I'm Ready' agreement, which enables the young person to stay on with their carer if both parties are happy with this.

Obviously you have no obligation to keep a young person in your household if you no longer want them to be there (as with any fostering situation), but as a long-term foster carer you need to be aware that young people may want and expect to remain with you beyond the age of 18. Once a young person is over the age of 18 their status changes and your role and financial situation in regard to them also changes, so this is something you may want to explore before committing to a foster placement that is planned to see a child into adulthood.

## Specialist fostering

Specialist fostering includes fostering for particular purposes, such as remand or treatment fostering.

• **Remand fostering** occurs in England and Wales, when young people are "remanded" by a court into the care of the local authority and placed with specially trained foster carers, as an alternative to custody, while they await trial or sentencing. In Scotland, young people may be placed in foster care as an alternative to placement in secure accommodation.

As a remand carer, you will normally be working with young people aged between 10–16, helping them to look at the causes of their offending behaviour, learn new ways of responding to stressful situations and managing their anger, and find new motivation and interests to replace those that led to them getting into criminal situations. Being a remand carer is demanding and you will need to work closely with the local youth justice system. It is also important to have experience of working with adolescents – either in your own family or in a professional capacity – and to be prepared to manage challenging behaviour. Remand carers usually work for specialist schemes where they receive targeted training and support, and appropriate financial remuneration for this demanding role.

• **Treatment fostering** is where experienced carers look after children and young people with complex needs and behavioural problems who are also receiving intensive support from other professionals.

## Short break

This is when disabled children or those with special needs or behavioural problems have a short stay with another family, while their own family or usual foster carers have a short break for themselves, or time to spend with their other children. This type of foster care may also be known as respite, family link or shared care – and different services may have different ways of referring to it.

It is important that the child coming to stay with you, either for a planned break or respite care, feels that they are not being "sent away", and people offering this sort of care usually try to ensure that the child gets some new experiences and happy memories from the visit. It is good to create a sense of occasion out of the child's visit and, where possible, plan some activities and new experiences (however small) that they might not have at home so the child feels welcomed in your family, and looks forward to visiting you.

## Parent and child

This is when a parent moves into a foster home with their child or children. These arrangements may involve an "assessment" of parents who have already had children removed from their care and where the risk is high that this will happen again; or may be purely to provide support and help for a young parent; or occasionally may reflect "pre-birth arrangements", where the mother is already living in the foster home.

> This young woman who came to me, she was that keen to keep her baby but she'd been through a rough time with her ex-boyfriend and this druggy crowd she'd got into. She knew she wanted a fresh start and to be a good mum. She's now got a job and is doing well for herself. She brings her little boy back to visit me whenever she can and she's met this lovely man and they're getting married next year.
> *Jeannie, experienced parent and child foster carer*

# 3

# Who can become a foster carer?

> Foster carers need to root for and be a champion for
> their young people – 'Come on, you can do this!' They
> need to offer physical and emotional support to help
> them reach their potential. Never set the bar too low –
> never underestimate what young people can achieve.
> *Rachel, recent care leaver*

## Are there age limits?

There are no official age limits for fostering. But a fostering service
will expect you to be mature enough to look after someone else's
child, and to work effectively with the child's family, social workers
and other professionals involved in their care. They will also expect
you to have a level of stability and security in your life, and to have
the health and stamina to be able to care for young children.

Grandparents can make excellent foster carers because of their
parenting and grandparenting experience, although the fostering
service will want to know that you are fit and well enough to
undertake the task.

## Do I need to be married?

All sorts of people become foster carers because children and young people have different requirements. Some children may thrive in a bustling two-parent family with other children, while others may need the individual attention of just one adult who can devote their time to them.

Fostering services are looking for people who can provide the stability, love and encouragement that individual children need and there is no "ideal" foster family – however much you may see stereotypes of foster families in TV dramas. That includes people who are single or living with a partner (cohabiting), as well as people who are married or divorced. If you are in a relationship (lesbian, gay or heterosexual), the service will want to make sure that the relationship is stable, so that you can provide security and continuity for fostered children.

If you are fostering alone, it's very important to have a good network of friends and/or family. This is essential because you will need to call on people to help out if you are ill or have to drop everything to be somewhere for the child or young person. You will also need people you can turn to for friendship, emotional support and a chance to unwind, when things aren't going so well.

> I was 29 with no man on the horizon and I knew I wanted children in my life. I'd worked in youth clubs and nurseries, been a nanny and worked with children in my role as a social worker. What I did know was that I didn't want a baby.
> *Annabelle, who fosters three girls, with support from her mother, brother and sister-in-law, quoted in 'If You Don't Stick with Me, who Will?'*

## I'm going to be doing most of the care. Will my partner also be a foster carer?

Some couples share equal responsibility for the care of foster children. However, in many situations one of the partners takes on most of the caring responsibilities and the other partner helps out for only part of the time, for example, if the former is at home and the latter is working full-time. However, the fostering service will want to be sure that both partners are able to provide high quality, safe care for children and that both are fully committed to the fostering task.

## What if I have children of my own?

Having your own children can be very valuable experience when it comes to fostering. But fostering is a role that the whole family takes on because it has a big impact on family life. It can be a positive experience for children to have foster siblings in the house, and many children say they have learnt a lot from it, but there may also be tensions over sharing toys and possessions, or time spent with parents. The fostering service will want to know that you have thought about this carefully, and they will talk to your children about their feelings. Some services run preparation groups and support networks for sons and daughters of foster carers. *We are Fostering* (Camis, 2003) is an interactive workbook and is helpful for children who foster (see Useful Reading)).

The fostering service will want to take into account the age of your own children as this may affect the age of children you foster. For example, some foster children will need to be the youngest in the family so they don't feel that they need to compete with others, and can get the attention they may never have received previously. In some cases, an abused child may pose a threat to younger children and it will be better if they are placed in a family where there are much older children or none at all. However, for some children being in a family with children of a similar age can be ideal, as this can help provide a stimulating environment where they have the chance to experience new activities and make new friends.

If you don't have children of your own, then it's important to have some experience of children before you consider becoming a foster carer. Fostering services are keen to recruit people who have professional experience, e.g. teachers, nursery workers, youth workers, social workers or care workers in residential homes, but they are also interested in people who have spent time caring for relatives' or friends' children, or who have worked with children as volunteers, e.g. running a Guide or Scout group, being a children's sports coach or volunteering with a charity for disabled children.

> One thing that people always ask about is the effect on my birth children, and what I say to them is that I didn't foster alone; we were a family that fostered. There were times when I felt guilty that my sons had to share me, but I believe that the fostering has turned them into much more rounded and caring adults.
> *Andy Hider, who has fostered over 80 teenagers across 26 years, quoted on www.corambaaf.org.uk*

## I have a health condition – can I foster?

Although fostering services encourage all types of people to consider fostering, it is important for fostered children to have a stable family life without any preventable disruption, such as a foster carer becoming seriously ill due to a long-term health condition. For these reasons, all prospective foster carers have a full medical examination carried out by their GP.

Being overweight, for instance, shouldn't affect your chances of becoming a carer, as long as it doesn't cause you to have serious health problems or impact on your ability to provide good care for a child.

## I'm a smoker – can I foster?

When a child goes to live with a foster carer, it is expected that those carers will do everything to safeguard the health and wellbeing of that child – and to set a good example. Different services have different policies about smoking – many may not accept smokers as carers for children under five, disabled children or children with asthma, but some will accept smokers who only smoke outside their home, as carers for older children/teenagers. Some will not accept smokers at all. If you smoke, you should discuss this with the fostering service.

## I'm disabled – will I be considered?

Yes. This will not automatically rule you out to foster a child. Many disabled people foster children, and some may feel that their experiences mean that they have gained skills that are ideal for fostering, such as strength and determination, or the ability to advocate for a child. Your social worker will discuss your impairment with you, including the impact, if any, that it has on your lifestyle and possible implications for parenting.

## Can I afford to foster?

You don't need to be well-off to be a foster carer – some carers are on benefits. As a foster carer, you receive an allowance to cover the cost of having a child living with you, so you should never be out of pocket.

Increasingly, fostering is being seen as a "professional" role and many fostering services now pay foster carers a fee on top of their allowance. This can be a reflection of the skills, abilities, length of experience or professional expertise the foster carer has or the extent of the child's needs.

## What if we don't own our home?

You don't need to own your own home to be able to foster.
However, you will need to prove that you have reasonable security
of tenure in order to provide continuity for the child. You also need
enough space for an extra child or young person, and to be able to
provide a separate furnished bedroom.

> I think it's good to have people who live in ordinary
> houses – not big posh places. Many of these children
> come from really poor housing and there can be a huge
> culture shock if they're suddenly in a ten-bed mansion
> with a swimming pool.
> *Deena, foster carer*

## Am I excluded from fostering if I have a criminal record?

There are some offences that mean you cannot be considered as a
foster carer, for example, if you have a conviction or caution under
Section 1 of the Sexual Offences Act 1956 (England and Wales), or
a conviction or caution for "crimes of violence" against children as
listed in Schedule 1 of the Children and Young People Act (England
and Wales) 1933. Offences are listed in the Fostering Services
Regulations 2011. Schedule 1 of the Criminal Procedure (Scotland)
Act 1995 gives information about offences that can bar people from
fostering in Scotland.

However, minor offences, especially those committed when you
were younger, won't necessarily prohibit you from fostering. But the
fostering service will need to know about these and consider them
carefully with your application. Everyone applying to foster has to
have a check of their criminal record, so it's a good idea to mention
any criminal convictions when you first apply to become a carer.

I certainly got in trouble when I was young, a bit of shoplifting and that kind of thing, but it was nothing major. I thought maybe that would count against me but our social worker said it could make me better able to relate to the kids, help them think about what they were getting into. They'd see from me that you don't have to make crime part of your life, you can lead a decent life with a job you like doing.
*Mike, foster carer*

## Do I have to be British?

You don't have to be a British citizen to foster in the UK, but you will probably need to prove that you have the right to be "domiciled" in the UK, i.e. the UK is your permanent home and you have the right to stay here permanently.

However, a service might consider someone who is here for a specific period of time, e.g. the partner of someone on a long-term work permit, if they could prove that they would be in the UK for enough time to undertake preparation and training and have children placed with them.

## Can I foster a child of a different ethnicity to me?

Studies show that children grow up best in a foster family that can help a child to develop an awareness of as many aspects of their culture, religion and ethnic origin as possible. This can help the child to have a positive sense of their own identity and heritage. Many foster carers do look after children of a different ethnicity to them, but you, your fostering service and the child's social worker will think carefully about how the placement will meet the child's sense of belonging and needs arising from their culture, religion and ethnic origin.

## What if we have pets?

Animals can be very helpful for children and young people who find it difficult to talk to other people about their feelings, or they can be a real "icebreaker" for a child who is finding it difficult to settle in new surroundings, helping them to feel like a member of the family. Dog ownership has also been correlated with good physical health.

However, there are also risks to having pets in the house, including safety issues such as being bitten, and some health or allergy risks, and for some children from particular religious or cultural groups, placement with a dog-owning family may not be appropriate. Also, some fostered children's behavior may pose a risk to pets, if they are unable to act appropriately around them, or tease or hurt them. Your fostering service will discuss your pets with you, and expect you to show that you are aware of any health and safety risks. Some services will undertake a pet assessment to look at possible issues.

> **Children who won't say a word to you will happily chat away to the dog, or spend ages cuddling the rabbit. It does help them to settle into our home.**
> *Fiona, foster carer*

**4**

# What sort of people make good foster carers?

> I remember being introduced to my new foster family
> and they said to the social worker, we're going on
> holiday in a couple of weeks and he has to come with
> us – can you arrange that? That was so amazing. I'd just
> met these people and they were, like, really determined
> to take me on holiday with them 'cos I was going to be
> part of their household, part of their family. It wasn't
> about them paying for the holiday – that was kind – but
> what really mattered to me was that they wanted to
> include me. That meant a lot.
> *Luke, young adult, fostered as a child*

Fostering services are looking for people who can provide safe,
secure and caring environments for children and young people who
are separated from their families. They need a wide range of people
because every child is different and children of all ages need foster
carers. They also need people from different walks of life, from
different cultures and communities, who can reflect and understand
a child's heritage, ethnicity, language and religion.

The role of a foster carer is to work in partnership with the fostering
service and other professionals to meet the child's care plan, which

may be to help prepare a child to return to their family, or to move on to adoption or whatever arrangements are made for the child's long-term needs. Therefore, fostering services need people who are willing and able to work as part of a team. You will work alongside social workers to implement care plans, to support children and their families to meet agreed goals. You will be asked to keep records, and take part in review meetings. You will get involved in many areas of the child's life, such as liaising with schools, taking children to medical or therapy appointments, or driving children to contact visits with family and friends.

## What are the key characteristics of foster carers?

To look after someone else's children, you need to really like the company of children and enjoy spending time with them – it may seem obvious but it's essential. Carers need to provide warmth, empathy and encouragement to children, to listen to them, encourage them, and make time to enjoy doing activities with them.

In addition, you need to recognise that many children and young people who need foster care have had very disturbing, unhappy and confusing experiences, and, on top of everything else, they will probably have mixed feelings about being separated from their families. You must also have plenty of patience and be prepared to get to know the child, and to try and understand the world from their point of view. You need to recognise that children will often have a lot of setbacks, and their progress towards change may be slow.

> I find it very rewarding to see a child who is so far away from their birth country and family blossom and grow in confidence...Being able to help a child settle and feel secure and safe. Giving them time to talk and helping them to learn everything from the language onwards. *Foster carer of unaccompanied asylum-seeking children,*

*quoted in 'Fostering Unaccompanied Asylum-Seeking
Young People'*

In your parenting of children, you need to be able to set boundaries
with fairness and empathy. Foster carers need to be able to
effectively manage often difficult behaviour, to set clear expectations
and be firm about structures and rules. When fostering as a couple,
there should be a shared approach to matters of discipline. Many
fostered children will have been exposed to neglect and/or abuse,
and this can affect their behaviour in many ways – they may have
eating disorders, insistently demand attention, be destructive or
particularly possessive with their belongings, have difficulties in
making relationships with others, or be overly fearful or bullying.
Some children will be affected by parental drug or alcohol misuse
or domestic violence, which can lead to, for instance, cognitive
difficulties, psychological problems or physical disabilities. Learning
how to manage behaviour like this and how to help and understand
the child is part of being a foster carer.

---

*Children in Care in England: Statistics* (Briefing Paper 04470,
5 October 2015) shows that in the year ending 31 March 2015,
out of a total of 69,540 children looked after at some time that
year by local authorities in England, 42,710 were in care
because of abuse or neglect.

---

You will need to be prepared to stick with children through difficult
times, with resilience and commitment, and to encourage and
support those who have low self-confidence and may be
disillusioned and angry. As someone who is expected to provide
stability and consistency, you will need to have your own life in fairly
good order, so you can provide a sense of routine and security for
children who may have come from chaotic backgrounds.

There are times I wake up and think what am I doing,
but I'm sure parents think that too. Being a foster carer
isn't for everybody, foster carers come from all different

walks of life and provide all sorts of things. It's a big commitment and it's difficult and challenging but it's important to be ready to identify the positive in things...even in the smallest of things. A child drops a plate but you have to recognise that the child was making the effort to put the plate in the sink. So you say thank you for doing that...or thank you for making your bed this morning, whatever else has gone wrong during the day...you can always find a positive.
*Theresa, therapeutic foster carer*

Children and young people have indicated the sorts of qualities they want in their foster carers (Sinclair, 2005). They want to be loved or liked in a way that is sensitive to their experiences and needs, and avoids conflicts of loyalty with their families. They value encouragement and attention; being listened to; given time; and made to feel that they count for something. Children and young people want to be accepted as part of the family, to get on well with other family members, and to feel that they have a place in that family. If they need to be disciplined (and some do accept the needs for rules and consequences), then they want discipline to be fair and consistent. Young people want a sense that their carer is not just doing it for the money, that they will stick with them and fight for them come what may and, particularly if they are in long-term foster care, that this commitment will outlast their official period of being in care.

These characteristics are mostly about interacting with and forming relationships with a child or young person, but successful fostering requires more than this. You will also need to be able to work effectively with others. This includes working well with other members of the fostering team – social workers, parents, schools and others. It needs empathy and a careful handling of the impact of these people on the child, as well as promoting the child's relationship with them. Many fostered children return home, and even if they don't, having contact with family and friends continues to be an important part of their lives. You'll need to understand why

children love their families – even if someone in that family has
seriously harmed or neglected them.

You'll need to have an understanding of identity and diversity – that
is, valuing the differences between people, and having a willingness
to learn about other cultures or issues appropriate to the children in
your care. It is about accepting individual children for who they are,
being non-judgemental, and being able to challenge discrimination
when appropriate. In an increasingly multicultural society, many
foster carers look after children of different ethnic or religious
backgrounds from their own, and do this very well. Foster carers
should have a flexible and open perspective to help them meet
children's needs.

Being a foster carer can be stressful, so fostering services provide
support to their carers, and it will be important that you can make
good use of this. However, more informal support, e.g. from family
and friends, will also be vital for practical and emotional help.

Foster carers come in all shapes and sizes, and so do children. What
makes a good foster carer for a disabled infant might be quite
different to what makes a good carer for a challenging teenager.

## Do I need to have certain skills?

You may hear the word "skills" used in connection with fostering,
but it often refers to the subjects explored above, or to practical
things like the ability to communicate well with a child or to see the
world through a child's eyes. Some people are good at encouraging
and praising children and making them feel valued and appreciated.
Other useful skills include being able to calm down a situation that
is getting out of hand, and helping a child channel their energy in
the right direction. You may have some of these skills already, and
others like them, through your own personal experiences. Others
can be gained through the training you receive as a foster carer.

You need to demonstrate that you can understand the requirements of fostering and do things like fill in a workbook to show this...but there are bound to be people who are really brilliant with children but are dyslexic and find that difficult, and fostering services must help you with this. Education is important, and you have to be prepared to help children with their education, but that doesn't mean you need a degree to do this work.
*Viv, foster carer*

Your fostering service will carry out an "assessment" of your abilities. They recognise that there will also be areas in which you feel less confident and need help to develop new skills. For example, you may need to learn more about how to manage challenging behaviour, how to care safely for children who have been sexually abused, or how to work with children's parents. This is why people interested in fostering take part in preparation courses, and in ongoing training if they go on to be approved as foster carers.

# 5

# Approaching a fostering service

I think I've fostered about 80 teenagers in total, and I'm still very passionate about it. To anyone thinking about foster care: maybe you've thought about it for years and are still sitting on the fence – it's that initial phone call that can be a difficult first step. But do pick up the phone – you're not committing yourself straight away and you've got to start somewhere! My best advice is to speak to another foster carer and hear about their experiences. Fostering has enhanced my life beyond anything else I've done and I wouldn't have it any other way.
*Andy Hider, who has fostered over 80 teenagers across 26 years, quoted on www.corambaaf.org.uk*

Becoming a foster carer can be a very rewarding experience, but it's a major commitment and it's important to think the process through very carefully. So you are advised to find out as much as possible about what fostering services are looking for in carers, and the needs of children who come into foster care. CoramBAAF publishes several books that will help you learn more (see Useful Reading).

## How the system works

It can be helpful to have some idea of how the fostering process works in the UK, so that you understand how services find foster carers, who you might be working with and how you might best use your skills.

- The local authority team or independent fostering service will recruit, approve and prepare foster carers ready to take on children and young people, when they are needed.

- Children taken into foster care are in the "care" of the local authority. This care may legally be shared with the child's parents, depending on the situation that brought them into care. You may hear the term "corporate parents" used to describe the responsibility local authorities have for children and young people in foster care. Part of this responsibility is about ensuring that the child lives with foster carers who are best able to meet the child's needs.

- The local authority has the responsibility for identifying a foster placement for a child. This may be done by a specialist family-finding team within the local authority who search within their in-house foster carers, but also contact IFPs to see if they have suitable placements to offer.

---

### SOCIAL WORKERS

All children who come into care should be allocated a social worker whose job is to ensure that the child's needs are met. The child's social worker is responsible for finding a fostering placement for the child – whether this is a short-term placement or a longer-term one.

As an approved foster carer, you will have your own supervising social worker in your fostering service.

---

I've met some brilliant social workers but I wouldn't do their job for all the tea in China ...there is so much criticism and people just don't understand the pressures they work under and the things they aren't allowed to talk about because of the need for confidentiality. In my opinion, you need a professional working relationship with your social worker – we don't necessarily have to be friends. That for me means first and foremost having a mutual respect and understanding for each other. Also we both have to have the same aim and you may have to argue that out – we may not always agree but we both have to be focused on the best interests of the child.
*Tee, specialist foster carer*

You can choose to foster for a local authority in your area, or an independent fostering service.

---

### TYPES OF SERVICE

**Local authority fostering services** (Health and Social Care Trusts in Northern Ireland) are usually based in the children's services, social services or social work department of a local authority. All children in care are "looked after" by a local authority.

**Other fostering services** are independent services (often shortened to IFPs) that are either run on a profit-making basis or a not-for-profit basis, sometimes with charitable status. Some may specialise in caring for children with complex needs.

---

## Where do I start looking for a fostering service?

These days it's hard to go far without coming across posters on bus stops or in train stations advertising for foster carers. You may also come across adverts in your local paper, displays in your local library, recruitment stalls in your local shopping centre, adverts in your local cinema and adverts on the internet and all forms of social media such as Twitter and Facebook. These may be for your local authority fostering service but also for IFPs. It is best to spend some time finding out about the different services that you could approach. Every fostering service is likely to have its own website giving details of the type of foster care they offer and what they are looking for in prospective foster carers. Local authorities may include their fostering team within their website or they may have a separate website for this.

---

**A good place to start looking for services in your area is on the internet – although you will also find details of fostering or "family-finding" services in your local phone book. The Fostering Network's website also has a search facility for fostering services (see www.thefosteringnetwork.org.uk). Most services work roughly within a 50 mile radius of their office.**

---

## Can I respond to adverts in my local paper or family-finding website for individual children?

When children and young people appear in local newspapers or on a family-finding website or magazine (such as *Foster Care*, published by Fostering Network), it is because their local authority is looking for a family who can offer the child or young person some sort of permanence. This might be with an adoptive parent or a long-term foster carer.

Before any child can join a foster or adoptive family, that family needs to be assessed and approved as suitable to care for children – this is a lengthy process. It will be in the best interests of the child if the local authority can find *someone who has already been approved*, and is now waiting to be matched to a child. So it's more common for people wanting to be foster carers to reply to these advertisements after they have been approved by a fostering service.

But it's always worth making enquiries if you feel that you could match the particular needs of a child or group of siblings, particularly if those needs are unusual or complex. You might be just the family that a service has been looking for, and they will be willing to take the time to assess your suitability for this child or sibling group.

## What should I consider when looking for a service?

It is important to find a fostering service that feels right for you. For some people it is very important to feel that they are contributing to their local community, so fostering for their local authority will be their first choice. Others may feel that they want to foster for a service that specialises in a particular type of need, for example, placing children with complex physical disabilities or children who have been remanded by the courts.

You might also want to look for a service that seems to need what you believe you are able to offer. For example, some might be keen to recruit carers for teenagers because they currently have enough carers for younger children. Others may be very short of black carers, or carers from particular ethnic backgrounds, or white carers, who can reflect the backgrounds of the children they need to place.

If you are approved as a foster carer, you will be working very closely with the service that approved you, and it's good to ensure that you find as good a "fit" as possible.

These are some of the questions you might want to bear in mind:

- Do they place the age group of children you are interested in fostering? For instance, babies are usually placed within local authority services.
- How local are they to you?
- How much support and training do they provide to their foster carers?

- What impression does the service make with you? How welcoming are they?
- What is their Ofsted rating?*
- Is fostering for your local authority important to you or would you prefer an independent service?
- What are your expectations in terms of financial remuneration (bearing in mind that fostering is not something you do for the money, but you do need to be able to pay your bills)?

You may have heard stories through the media about people who approach a fostering service and feel that their initial response is not encouraging. Sometimes this is because in a large organisation, such as a local authority, your call can get re-routed to the wrong person, or the phone gets answered by a temporary staff member, who doesn't fully understand the importance of their role in welcoming prospective carers. However, increasingly all services are becoming very aware of the need to give prospective carers a good welcome and to encourage them. So if you don't get the response you expect, it is worth giving them a second chance and being very clear about why you are interested in fostering and what you believe you have to offer. If you still don't feel this is the right service for you, then there are others who will be happy to welcome you.

## Contacting a service

Most fostering services will have a website where you can get a good feel for what they are looking for. They often have a form for making an online enquiry. You can also call and ask them about the types of foster carers they are looking for, how the service works and what types of fostering they do. Alternatively, you might want to respond to advertisements you see locally or as part of national recruitment campaigns.

* Ofsted is the Office for Standards in Education, Children's Services and Skills. It inspects and regulates services that care for children and young people, including fostering services, and services providing education and skills for learners of all ages, and rates their performance.

Every service has their own process for responding to people who contact them. You may be sent an information pack or asked to fill out an online form, or a staff member may call to have a chat about what they are looking for. They will be interested in knowing more about you, your family and your home, and will help you to consider if fostering is right for you.

Many fostering services hold open evenings or information events, and you may be invited to attend, especially if there is one scheduled in the near future. It's a good idea to do so, because it's an opportunity to hear more about how the service works and to meet people who are already fostering.

> It's the other foster carers who bring it alive for you.
> They tell what it's like to have these children in your
> house with you, day in and day out. They've got a way
> of looking at it like nobody else has 'cos they are the
> ones who are living that experience. You come across
> stuff that you've never thought about before and that
> can stop you in your tracks. Sometimes you just need to
> think about it and talk it through with your partner, but
> it could also be something that makes you go, hey, this
> really isn't something that's going to work for us as a
> family.
> *Jason, foster carer*

The next step is to meet with a social worker from the service to consider this further, and to answer any questions that you may have. For example, if you are worried that you might not be able to afford to foster, then ask about the financial side of things. If you are worried that a criminal conviction might stand in the way, tell the social worker at this early stage.

Once you have been in contact with a service, and if you and the service agree that you might be suitable to foster, you will usually complete an application form. You will also be asked to give permission for the service to carry out criminal records checks (in England and Wales, called Disclosure and Barring Service, or DBS, checks; in Scotland, called Disclosure Scotland checks), so that they can ensure that you and anyone living with you do not have a conviction for offences against children, and that a child will be safe living with you. You will also be asked to have a health check to show that you don't have any major health problems that would make it difficult for you to look after children. The names and details of people who are prepared to give references for you will also be needed.

If at any stage you decide that fostering isn't what you expected, or the service's approach doesn't feel right for you, speak to your social worker. Never be afraid to say if you don't want to go ahead – fostering isn't right for everyone, or it may not be right at that particular time in your life. Some people drop out of the process, but then come back to fostering later in their lives, when their circumstances have changed.

## Do services have to assess me as a foster carer?

No: if a service feels that what you can offer does not meet the types of children they need to place, then they do not have to assess you. Their resources are limited so they must concentrate on what is needed by children in their area. For example, if you are very clear that you will only consider taking a baby or pre-school age child, and the service places older children, this will not be ideal for either of you.

# 6

# Preparation and assessment

Once your application has been accepted by the fostering service, you will start the preparation and assessment process. This can take about six to eight months, sometimes longer, but your social worker should keep you informed.

## The preparation group

During the assessment process, you will attend a series of preparation and training sessions to learn more about fostering, along with other people who are applying. You will have a chance to hear from experienced foster carers, and to learn about a range of issues, including:

- why children come into care and need to be fostered;
- issues of loss, separation and trauma and how children feel when separated from their family;
- attachment issues and how a poor experience of attachment affects behaviour;
- managing difficult behaviour;
- contact and working with parents;
- child protection and how to provide "safe care";

- working in partnership with social workers and others as part of a team;
- helping children move on and the importance of being prepared to say "goodbye".

## SAFE CARE

Safe care is the term used to describe ways of looking after children and young people that protect the child or young person from situations that may remind them of times when they have been abused, or that they may misinterpret as being abusive. Safe care is also about the carer making sure that they protect themselves from a child or young person making allegations against them by carefully considering their actions in order to avoid this kind of misunderstanding. Foster carers are taught about safe care as part of their preparation and training.

The social workers running the sessions generally prepare a brief report on your participation in the group, which you should be able to see and comment on. It will be part of the information used in the final assessment report.

> The preparation group was much better than we'd imagined. It was good to be in the same boat as other people, all of us not really knowing what to expect and being able to talk about things without feeling like you were getting it wrong or asking stupid questions. We've stayed friends with one of the couples we met in the group.
> *Savita, foster carer*

If you are in England, you will almost certainly be introduced to the Training, Development and Support Standards (TSDS) for Fostering, which give a framework for your ongoing training and professional development. They cover an understanding of the principles and values essential for fostering, your role, health and safety, communications, understanding of children's development, keeping children safe and your development as a foster carer.

Sometimes you will be provided with a TSDS workbook to use with your social worker to complete work on the standards within 12 months of starting work as a foster carer. You can see an example of this at: www.gov.uk/government/publications/training-support-and-development-standards-for-foster-care-evidence-workbook. Achieving the standards is not just about attending courses – examples of meeting everyday challenges can also be used to demonstrate the required skills and knowledge.

Other parts of the UK may not use the same format, but will have their own approaches to ensuring how you as a foster carer will be supported and have access to training, especially in the first year. These will cover very similar aspects to those mentioned above.

## The assessment process, or "home study"

Alongside this preparation, you will be visited by a social worker at home, and perhaps meet at their office, usually eight to ten times. They will meet with you individually as well as together, if you are a couple, and will also want to talk to your own children, if you have them. This is how the fostering service gets to know you and assesses your suitability to be a foster carer. It is also how you learn about what will be involved and consider, with the social worker, whether you have the necessary skills and strengths. The social worker will help you to think about your life experiences, your knowledge of caring for children, the skills you could bring to the task, and how you will work as part of a team. They will also discuss additional training or support that you may need. If you have children, they will be asked about their feelings about the family fostering, and may be invited to special preparation groups. You will need to be open and honest, as the social worker needs to know your limitations (everyone has some) to make sure that suitable help is provided and that you can be matched with a child whose needs you can meet.

The same social worker will meet and talk with your personal referees. Information from your referees and criminal record and health checks is important as it will help them to back up the points that they make in their assessment report.

# What exactly will the assessment cover?

## Background information, history and individual profiles

The social worker will explore with you your family background, experience of being parented and your relationship with siblings, if any. As part of this, they will probably ask you to do a family tree, showing your parents, grandparents and siblings. The social worker will also ask you to put together a chronology, or a list with dates, of the places where you have lived and of important life events. They will also ask about your educational and employment history.

The point of this is to build up an accurate account of your family and life experiences so far. However, in addition to this, they also want to explore with you how your experiences have made you into the person you now are and how they are likely to affect the sort of foster carer you will be. The social worker is not necessarily looking for a problem-free background. In fact, having worked through earlier traumatic experiences and come out the other side can be an important strength. What is important is that past events have been fully processed or accepted, rather than continuing to affect you unhelpfully.

> I think you need to have experience to be a foster carer.
> I'm sure there are people who've had a so-called "ideal
> life" who make perfectly good foster carers, so I
> wouldn't take that away from them, but I do feel that
> myself and my partner, we've experienced probably

> ninety per cent of things that they have experienced when they come to us, either as children or as adults.
> *Foster carer, quoted in 'Who am I and what do I do?'*

The social worker will also want to explore your friendships and influences outside your family. They will discuss with you how you see yourself in terms of ethnicity, class, gender, sexuality and religious faith, if any. Experiences of discrimination and racism may have been important for you and will need to be discussed. Even if you haven't experienced these, what understanding do you have of them? Your views on what can lead some parents to neglect or abuse their children will be relevant, as this may be the situation from which foster children will come. Finally, the social worker will want to learn about your interests and hobbies and the sorts of things you are looking forward to doing with foster children.

### Current relationship

If you are planning to foster as a couple, the quality, stability and permanence of your relationship will be important. Fostering a child may put stress on your relationship and you should think about how you will work together and support each other. The social worker will be interested in how you have resolved difficulties in the past and how you communicate when things are not going well. They will also want to learn about the strengths in your relationship.

> We thought we had an honest, open relationship with no secrecy, but as it turned out we didn't even know what we weren't being honest about. There were some very important things we had never discussed. We're not so smug now, but we are far more open and we're also a much closer family. We value each other more than we did because our relationships have been close to breaking point.
> *Foster carer, quoted in 'Could you be my Parent?'*

## Family lifestyle – roles and relationships

Every family is different – family rules and habits, traditions, ways of expressing feelings. There may be roles that members have taken on in your family, for instance, the joker, the organiser, the baby, etc. The social worker will want to learn about how your family operates and discuss with you how this is likely to change when you are fostering. They will want to explore how flexible all members of the family are, as the impact of a child will depend partly on their needs and personality and cannot be foreseen completely. They will want to know what commitments you have in relation to any children already in your family. They will often ask you to write about a typical week or weekend and reflect on how this will change when you have a foster child.

## Parenting skills

The social worker will talk with you about your experience with children and your approach to caring for them. If you already have children, you will have discovered what works for you and how to tailor this to the different personalities of your children. If you don't yet have children, you may have experience of being with them, or may need to gain such experience. Your social worker will be able to make suggestions about this. You may well already have valuable experience of working with children, either on a paid or voluntary basis, so through this, and your experience of being parented yourself, you will have views on how you may set boundaries and forms of discipline you might use.

A child joining your family may have experienced very poor parenting at home. You will need to discuss with your social worker, and perhaps with other experienced carers, how this may have affected their behaviour. You may need to consider new parenting skills to help the child to unlearn the ways in which they adapted to the poor parenting they received earlier.

You will need to discuss with the social worker practical arrangements for caring for a child, particularly if you currently work full time. Depending on the sort of fostering you plan to do and the requirements of your service, you may or may not be able to combine fostering with other paid work.

> Throughout the assessment we were treated as individuals, it focused on what we'd done before, the strengths we might have to look after children, as well as the difficulties.
> *Justin and Dan, quoted in 'Recipes for Fostering'*

## Support networks, using support and problem-solving skills

As a foster carer, you should be given good support by your service. You will have your own supervising social worker, and you will be offered and expected to attend training sessions. There will also probably be a local foster carers' support group. The social worker will want to discuss the importance of working as a member of the team around a child and using support from the service.

The social worker will also be interested in your own current support networks and your experience of using support from your family, friends and community. Are you involved in giving support, perhaps to elderly parents, or to adult children or grandchildren, and how will this be managed when you start fostering?

## Motivation and expectations

You will need to think about your reasons for wanting to foster. Fostering can be a career; however, it won't usually provide a guaranteed source of income as this will depend, in the main, on foster children being in placement. If you already have children, you will need to think about how they and a foster child will affect each other. It will be helpful if you can talk to experienced foster carers and learn about the particular emotional and behavioural issues that children who need fostering are likely to have, and that may make fostering very different from your initial expectations. You will also need to consider the likely impact on you and your family of the involvement you may have with the families of fostered children.

## Strengths and limitations

All prospective foster carers have a variety of strengths and limitations. The assessment process should give you the opportunity to identify and discuss these with your social worker. He or she can suggest ways in which you can start to address limitations by, for example, starting to develop your support network. It will be important that your strengths and limitations are described honestly in the assessment report as this will help in identifying children whose needs you could meet and the kind of placement support you will need. If you are working with the TSDS Standards, a personal professional development plan will be agreed with you and worked on over your first year of fostering.

> If my home-grown children were being looked after by someone else, then I would want the very best for them and that is why it is so important to accept all the training on offer; we are looking after other people's children.
> *Chris, foster carer*

# Will they ask very personal questions?

The social worker will want to build up a picture of you and your family (if you have one). They will want to know what is important to you, and the experiences that have made you into the person you are. They may ask about intimate areas of your life such as your personal history and your relationships because this can be relevant to how you care for a child. This might seem very intrusive, but you have to try and see it from their point of view. You might be asked to think about a recent bereavement you have had and how you will cope with a child who has experienced major losses in their life. Or if you and your family tend to walk about the house with very few clothes on, you will be asked to consider the effect on a child who has been sexually abused. You might also be asked to think about what advice you would give to a young person who thinks they are gay, lesbian or bisexual, or who is under the age of consent and having sex.

They will also need to know that there are no issues in your own past that might be triggered while caring for a child. This does not mean that people who have experienced abuse in their own childhoods are ruled out as foster carers, but that services need to know that you have received support to help you manage these issues.

> Deep inside, I think I knew I was not being entirely honest but I told myself that a few isolated incidents in my childhood could not possibly be relevant 25 years later. I had given my husband a sketchy account of these earlier in our relationship, but neither of us mentioned them as we answered all the social worker's questions and waited anxiously for the outcome of the assessment. When asked if there were any background issues or characteristics we did not feel we could manage, we said that we thought we could manage anything, except perhaps a significant physical disability.
>
> When we were introduced to four-year-old Melanie and her baby brother, we were thrilled. We were told that it was likely that Melanie had witnessed sexual activity in her mother's care but in the excitement of introductions, we chose not to ask more about this. She was so little and so delightful, what could possibly be the problem...

> By the time Melanie started to tell us what had
> happened to her in her mother's house, I was beside
> myself with shock and horror. I wanted to focus on
> Melanie and our new family but found myself thrown
> back into the past. I had not thought about my paternal
> grandfather very much at all since his death but now
> memories came flooding in...
> *Quote from 'Parenting a Child Affected by Sexual
> Abuse'*

It's much better to get issues out into the open and think about
how you would deal with them at this stage, rather than wait until
later on when they might cause problems. But if you do find some
of these matters really difficult to discuss (for example, because, in
your culture, these issues are never discussed with strangers),
explain this to the social worker. You can ask for time to think about
the issues, or ask the social worker to be more specific about why
they need to know this information.

## Why is this process necessary?

All children needing foster care will have experienced separation
from their family. Many will have experienced further losses, or
neglect and abuse. They are, understandably, likely to be demanding
to care for and, for their sake and yours, it is important that you are
well prepared. The preparation and assessment process should also
give you and the service an opportunity to recognise your needs,
strengths and limitations. It will be intrusive and demanding but
should also be thought-provoking and stimulating. Regulations set
out the information that the fostering service is required to gather
and the issues it has to address. You can look at these for yourself
by visiting the foster care section of www.gov.uk/dfe. Further
information about standards across the UK can be found via the
relevant government websites.

## Checks and references

When you applied to foster, you will have been asked to give permission for the checks that the service is required to carry out (see p 44). This is usually done while the assessment process is happening. It involves checks of criminal records on all members of your household aged 18 or over (16 or over in Scotland; 10 or over in Northern Ireland). Checks will also be made of the local authority where you live and sometimes where you have lived for the last five or ten years (or sometimes longer). Your current employer will usually be contacted, to verify employment dates, your role and whether there have been any relevant disputes or disciplinary proceedings.

If you work or have worked with children or vulnerable adults, the social worker may need to contact the employer for more details. If you know of anything that will be revealed by these checks, it is vital that you discuss this immediately, before the checks are done. Your openness in doing this and your explanation of the circumstances will be helpful and will demonstrate that you can work well in partnership with the service and have the courage to address difficult issues. Any attempt to conceal information will be of great concern and may lead the service to question whether they can work with you. They must feel confident that they can trust you to be responsible, as you will be caring for vulnerable children on their behalf.

## Personal referees: who should I choose and what will be expected of them?

All parts of the UK have regulations and minimum requirements about references. These are immensely helpful in building up a picture of you and the possible impact of fostering on you and your family. The service should explain early on about the number and range of referees and what they might expect in writing and through talking to them. It is important to choose people who know you well and, if possible, have done so for some time.

More than two referees may be needed as it is important to have people who have known each of you for some time, if you are a couple, as well as people who know you both as a couple and people who have fairly frequent contact with you now. It would be helpful if your referees know something of what fostering will involve and you may want to give them some of the written material that the social workers have given you. They will be asked about their relationship with you; the stability and permanence of your relationship with each other, if you are a couple; your experience with children; how you will understand and manage a child's behaviour, and respond to the child's need to remain in touch with their family. They will be asked about any concerns they may have about the safety of a child placed with you and the support they think you may need. The information they provide may or may not be shared with you.

## What if I don't get on with my social worker or want to change service?

It is important that there is a trusting relationship between you and your social worker(s). You need to be able to discuss issues, some of which may be difficult, with openness and honesty. In the majority of cases, this can be achieved. However, if you feel this isn't working, and you have tried without success to resolve the situation with your worker, you could ask for a meeting involving his or her manager. If this doesn't help, you could ask for a change of social worker and this may be able to be arranged. However, the reality is that most fostering teams are quite small and this may be difficult to arrange or may involve a delay.

A change of service part-way through an assessment is fairly drastic, although it can be done. It would involve firstly discussing this with your current service before finding another one willing to accept your application. It might be possible for some of the work done already to be transferred but it might be that the new service would want to start from the beginning. The new service would need to talk with the original workers as well as with you about why the first assessment had to stop. It is not possible to be approved by more than one service (except in very rare instances in Scotland) although, once approved, children from other services can be placed with you.

## A second opinion

Some services routinely have another social worker, often a senior or manager, who will meet with you towards the end of the assessment process. They will discuss further with you any issues that seem to them to be still outstanding or to need further clarification. This is also an opportunity for you to comment on the assessment and highlight any further training that you feel would be helpful.

## The assessment report

Your social worker will record information about you as part of this process, and put together a report, often using CoramBAAF's Form F. This gives details of your skills, and your social worker's recommendations about the age of children or type of fostering that they feel will best suit you. They will also include details of any areas where they feel you will need extra support. You will be able to see this report and add your own comments, and to raise any points that you disagree with, or to amend incorrect facts.

> We had a very good assessment process and the social worker we dealt with was extremely considerate and empathetic, she wanted to let us go through the process ourselves. Rather than putting the process on us, she let us talk and guided us, and my husband, who is quite a box-ticker, found that more difficult – but she was more interested in hearing how we interacted and dealt with things and talked about things together.

> When we got the report through there were two tiny
> mistakes on dates but the rest was so good, so accurate
> – we felt really listened to. And my husband said they
> 'get us, they understand us'. We felt really held by that
> process.
> *Philippa, foster carer*

## Going to panel and being approved

> Going to panel is nervewracking – you can't say it's not.
> But you have to remind yourself, if that was my child
> being placed with strangers, I'd want someone to put
> them through the wringer – make sure they were going
> to be the right sort of people.
> *Meena, foster carer*

Your social worker will present their report to a fostering panel.
Most fostering services have their own panel, although some may
share it with another service. A panel is a group of people with a
combination of professional and personal experiences of fostering. It
may include very experienced social workers; foster carers or people
who have grown up in foster care; and representatives from the
local community, such as councillors. Panels will also have access to
legal and medical advisers to help in the decision-making process.

The panel receives a copy of your assessment report before the
meeting so they have time to consider it carefully. The panel
respects the confidentiality of applicants and will only discuss
relevant information with other panel members during the meeting.
At the meeting, they discuss what you can offer as well as any
concerns they may have. Your assessing social worker will attend to
answer any questions. It is usual for applicants to be invited to
attend the panel.

After their discussion, the panel will make a recommendation to a
senior member of the fostering service – the decision-maker. This

person will make the decision as to whether or not to approve you, taking into account the panels' recommendation, and will write to you with this and the terms of your approval, if any. The large majority of carers who get to this stage are approved. However, if you are not approved, you can accept this and withdraw; or ask the decision-maker to review the proposed decision; or apply, if your service is in England or Wales, for an independent review.

## Independent review

If you are not approved and your service is in England or Wales, you have 28 calendar days to decide whether to apply for an independent review. An Independent Review Mechanism (IRM) operates in England, and the IRM Cymru in Wales. It is only the proposal not to approve you that you can ask to be reviewed at this stage, not any terms and conditions of your approval. If you apply, arrangements will be made for your case to be considered by an independent panel, which will make a recommendation to your service about your suitability as a carer. The decision-maker must consider this carefully before making his or her final decision. In other parts of the UK, services have procedures to review an adverse decision if you request this.

If you are still unhappy and feel you have been unfairly treated, you may have the right to make use of the service's complaints procedure.

## Can I apply again or to another service?

If your circumstances change substantially, it may be appropriate for you to apply again, or you may want to apply to another service that needs foster carers for different types of children or situations. For example, some services particularly need carers to provide "short break" care – where carers have children to stay with them at weekends or for holiday periods – and so may not be concerned if you have some important time commitments, so long as you can be available at certain times. Services may ask whether you have applied elsewhere, and it is expected that you will be honest with them about any reasons you have been given for being turned down.

# 7

# Being a foster carer

> We have a great relationship with our [supervising]
> social worker. Feeling valued is so important – my local
> authority is very good at that, and we feel we are
> involved in decisions. They listen to you. The decision
> may not be what you want it to be, but if you've felt
> listened to and valued, then you're much less likely to
> feel disgruntled.
> *Pip, foster carer*

Fostering is about working in partnership with social workers, as
well as teachers, medical staff, therapists and anyone else involved
in planning for the child's future and helping the child.

## Who will I be working with?

### Supervising social worker

Once you are approved, you will have a supervising social worker
(also sometimes known as a link worker or support worker), who
will support you in looking after children. They will make sure that

you have any additional training or equipment that is needed to care for a child.

> **We can get this idea that as foster carers we have to get it right, all the time. That we should somehow always know what to do, that if we admit we don't know or we've got a problem, that the service won't use us any more – but that's ridiculous. Every child is different and you're always coming across new situations, so you will make mistakes. We're only human and it's best to admit that, and ask for help if you need it.**
> *Adrian, foster carer*

Once a child is with you, your supervising social worker will contact you regularly, and visit you, to see how you are getting on, and discuss the child's progress. This will be to offer you support, and also to make sure you are fulfilling your part of the plans for the child's future. Information from these visits will be recorded. Every foster carer also has to have an annual review where the service reviews your approval as a foster carer, and checks that you are working within the regulations and Standards every service has to follow, and within any local policies or practices they want you to observe. It's also an opportunity for you and the service to recognise the new skills you've gained and the positive work you've been doing with children. It's a time to look at whether you are ready to take on more complex or challenging children, or if there are particular areas where you'd like to develop your knowledge and experience.

## Child's social worker

Children who come to stay with you will also have their own social worker. They should tell you as much as possible about the child or young person's daily routines, cultural or religious practices, dietary needs, etc, before the child moves in with you. They make arrangements for the child to visit family members (where appropriate), and resolve any problems arising from this. The child's social worker also prepares the child (if the child is old enough) for meetings where plans for their future will be discussed, and helps the child to express their thoughts and feelings about this. The social worker will attend the meetings with the child, and you will also be included in these. The child's social worker has to make sure that the child or young person has information about being in foster care, has opportunities to express their opinions and concerns, that their education and health are being looked after, and that they have access to leisure and career opportunities. You will also be expected to keep a confidential record of the child's progress with you and any events that affect them or their care, and to hand over these records to the child's social worker when the child leaves you.

If the young person is coming up to the age of leaving foster care, they should be helped to prepare for life as a young adult, and they may be allocated a social worker who specialises in preparing children who are leaving care.

**We try to point out to foster carers that if they want to be treated as professionals, then you must behave professionally. When you put in reports for meetings, it's important to allow enough time for people to respond. It's an emotional role being a foster carer and at times it is important to step back and look at the issues and not take our own feelings into account, and remember what is in the best interest of the child.**
*Steve Stockley, Fosterline Manager, also foster carer and adopter*

## Other foster carers

You may also receive support from experienced foster carers. In some services, experienced carers "mentor" new foster carers. In many areas there are also fostering support groups where you can meet other carers to exchange ideas and maybe do some fun things together – like taking children out for the day as part of a large group, or holding parties and barbeques.

> Having other carers to talk to is so helpful. You come across a behaviour or some problem that hasn't come up before, and then you talk to one of the more experienced carers and they say, 'Oh we had something like that – and we tried x or y'. They can give you ideas you haven't thought about before, it's that reassurance of knowing someone else has experienced this, someone else has found a way through it.
> *Viv, foster carer*

## Other people you may work with

You may also work closely with the child's teachers and other specialist staff from the school or education authority – such as the Special Educational Needs Co-ordinator (SENCO) or designated teacher (someone appointed by the school to look after the needs of children in care). You may need to help school staff understand the difficulties your foster child has, which may be causing behavioural problems. You may also be working alongside health professionals such as GPs, nurses and hospital consultants, and speech and language therapists. If a child has experienced a lot of emotional trauma and disruption, they may also need to see a therapist or counsellor. You may be asked to take part in progress meetings with the therapist.

If there is a court hearing about your foster child, you may meet the children's guardian (England and Wales) or curator *ad litem* (Scotland), who is appointed by the court to safeguard the interests of the child. They may be interested in your opinions about the child and what is best for them.

> As a carer you need to be pushing for kids to reach their maximum potential in education, as in all aspects

of their life – in whatever way that may be. I recently
had a child turned down for a special needs school. This
was a child who'd been abused for many years. She was
elective mute, hyper-mobile, hyper-vigilant and globally
delayed by two years – but she was being expected to
cope in a mainstream school. It's so important to me
that I fight to get these children the right place in
education – this is about their future.
*Theresa, therapeutic foster carer*

## What about the child's parents?

Often fostering is about providing somewhere safe for the child to
live while their family receives help to sort out their problems. This
might mean the parent having time to separate from an abusive
partner, or demonstrate their ability to live without misusing drugs
or alcohol, or for a family to think about how they will keep the
child safe in the future. It may be a chance for a stressed parent
who had little love and support in their own childhood to learn
more about how to care for their child. In all these cases, it will be
important for the child to continue to have contact with their
family so that they will be able to return home as soon as the
parents are ready to care for them again, and you may be asked to
take the child to meetings with their parent in a contact centre.
The child's parents and maybe other members of the child's family
will usually be involved in some of the meetings about planning the
child's future.

We did discover that when the mum did turn up for
contact visits, she always tried to get Nicola alone. She'd
then tell Nicola that she shouldn't talk to us, shouldn't
tell us anything, that she would soon be back and living
with her. We couldn't say anything negative to Nicola
about her mum and we couldn't risk having any kind of
confrontation with her mum in front of Nicola, but we
knew Nicola had lots of worries that she needed to

share with us. So we'd say to Nicola, 'Mummy is upset because she can't be with you all the time, and she is saying things that under normal circumstances she wouldn't say. But you have to talk to us about any upsets and anxieties that are worrying you – it wouldn't be fair on you to wait a whole month to tell your mum.' That was the way we got round it and it was quite successful.

*Robin and Louise, quoted in 'If you don't stick with me, who will?'*

# 8

# Caring for children in your home

> Our own children have grown through dealing with this...We always involve them in the decisions and we talk at the end of a placement about what we could have done better. Our children have to make some compromises that other children don't make...but that's how we live.
> *Pip, foster carer*

Once you have been approved, you may find yourself caring for a child almost immediately, or there may be a time gap because the fostering service doesn't have a child whom they need to place just at the moment.

## What happens when my service wants me to take a child?

In most cases you will be contacted and asked to consider taking a particular child – or sibling group, if you are approved to take siblings – who needs fostering, and whom the service thinks that you and your family can care for well. You will be given an outline of the child or young person's circumstances and the problems and issues they are likely to have. If you are prepared to take this child, then the child's social worker may contact you and give you more information about their daily routines, their school, the types of food they eat, and any medical or special needs they have, or it may be that your initial contact has given you this information already.

You will also be told basic information about the child or young person's relationship with members of their own family and whether the child will have contact with them while they are with you. You should be told a bit about what you will be expected to do to meet the needs of the child.

Ideally, children's moves into foster care are planned; in other words, they are discussed beforehand and the child's family is aware of what is happening. This means that social workers are also able to prepare you, as the foster carer, to look after the child. However, often children come into care on an "emergency" basis. This may be because children are found at home on their own at night; the child's parent is rushed into hospital; the parent is arrested; or the child is considered to be at serious risk of imminent harm. The social worker may know very little about the child in these cases and you will have to apply your training and skills to provide the most appropriate care, until more is known. The child's social worker should keep in regular contact with you, and your supervising worker will be available for additional support.

## What if I don't think this child will fit in with my family?

If, when you are asked if you are able to take the child, you feel that this child or young person isn't right for your family, or you feel that there are aspects of the child's needs that you don't feel skilled enough to cope with, you should tell your social worker. They may be able to offer you extra training or support to help you care for the child. You do not have to take any child that you feel you cannot care for, and it is irresponsible to take a child whose needs you cannot meet, as the placement is likely to disrupt prematurely.

> You get to say yes or no, nobody is making you take these children. You say what you think will fit with your household and then you discuss with the placement team...Then you have a discussion with your social worker and you think about what you can do practically and you have to be flexible – which is a big skill for foster carers. And it's brilliant – not that it hasn't been hard. We have times we sit there and think what are we doing, but other times the resilience of some of these kids is amazing, and has taught us so much.
> Stuart, foster carer

## How much information will I get about the child?

When you are approached to take on a child, you should be given enough information about them and their situation to enable you to make an informed decision about whether you have the skills and right environment to take this child. Once the child is with you, there will be a placement meeting during which more detailed information about the child or young person's situation will be shared so you can understand your role in the child's care. For example, you may be asked to help a child learn to play, to observe the interaction between a sibling group, or to help a child learn to manage their anger. After the placement meeting you should be given a placement agreement, setting out what has been agreed. The child's social worker should keep in contact with you, and your supervising worker will be available for additional support, and to review how things are going.

## Welcoming a child to your home

Children may be very confused and frightened when they first come to you – especially if their move into care has been a sudden one. But even if it has been planned, the child may still be very upset or angry. Children may have strong feelings about their own families, and even if other adults feel that the child's parents have let them down or harmed them, most children will be unhappy to be away from them. They may also be worrying about brothers or sisters who are still at home, or they may be concerned about a parent who, for example, has a drug or alcohol problem. But some children will arrive seeming very confident and relaxed. They may have been in foster care before and know what to expect!

Your preparation to become a foster carer will help you to think about these issues and how you will welcome a child and help them to settle in your home. Experienced foster carers say that it's important to take time to show the child or young person around your home, and explain to them where things are and any routines or rules that you and your family have. Depending on their age, you may need to explain how to go to the bathroom at night, if they need a nightlight, who to ask if they need a drink, rules around mealtimes, and about bathing, changing and washing clothes. Girls may not know how to manage their period in your house. Many carers have spare toys, clothes and toiletries in case children or young people have come without their own. If you have children of your own, they often help a new child to settle in. Pets can also be a great way of helping children to relax.

## Emotional needs

Many fostered children have been through difficult times and some may be traumatised by their experiences. Their self-confidence is often low and they may have worries about the future. Some children will receive professional help from a therapist or psychologist, and many children will have support and help from their social worker. As a foster carer, you will be expected to help the child to talk about their memories, fears and worries – as well as to remember good things in their lives. You may find yourself doing life story work (sometimes called life work) with a child, where you help the child to put together a book about their past, or put together a "memory box". This may include photos or drawings of the people and places that are important to them, to help them make sense of what has happened in their lives. CoramBAAF has a number of resources on this subject (see Useful Reading).

Much of your "work" will be around getting to know the child or young person, so that they feel comfortable talking to you. Only then will you be able to help them think about ways to tackle problems that are worrying them. You will also help to build up the child or young person's self-esteem by offering encouragement and giving lots of praise when they achieve things, however small.

## Will children disclose abuse to me?

Sometimes very little will be known about what has actually happened to the child before they came into foster care, and while social workers may suspect that the child has been harmed, they may have no actual knowledge as to whether physical or sexual abuse has occurred.

Sometimes children will "disclose" to you abuse that has happened to them. They may do this through actual words, but hints of their experiences may also come out through their play or through interactions with other children – which is why it is so important that foster carers keep records of children's behaviour. Some children may also have "flashbacks" to traumatic past events.

As part of your foster carer training, you will learn how to react and how to help children when they talk about abuse, how to handle inappropriate behaviour and what to do if children have flashbacks. You will also be trained how to provide "safe care" so that children do not become distressed by situations that might trigger memories of abusive situations, or misinterpret innocent actions as something sexualised or threatening. You will also be

given advice on how to keep records of any information that you
need to pass on to the child's social worker.

Hearing about a child's past trauma can be very distressing and you
need to ensure that you have support for yourself. Don't be afraid
to discuss your support needs with your supervising social worker.

> I've heard some really distressing stuff, but my distress is
> nothing compared with what these children have been
> through. You have to try and hide your own sense of
> shock, while making it clear to the child that you
> absolutely believe them and that you totally believe
> that no child should ever be treated in that way – and
> that none of this is in any way their fault.
> *Margot, foster carer*

## Behaviour management

Some of the children you care for may seem just like any other child
– well behaved some of the time, difficult some of the time and
somewhere in the middle for the rest! But many fostered children
and young people will have challenging behaviour that they need
help with. They may be quiet, withdrawn and anxious. They may
self-harm by cutting themselves, or starve themselves, or binge on
food. Or they may "fly off the handle" at the slightest provocation,
get into fights with other children, or regularly get into trouble at
school or with the police. You may find that things get broken in
your house, by accident or because the child has never been taught
how to play, or because they are upset and break things.

> I don't try to get them to change really. I think if you
> can show the child, regardless of how much they're
> flinging at you, an acceptance, a knowledge – 'I know
> what you're doing is really rotten but I can understand
> why you're doing it. I can't change it but maybe I can
> help you accept it.' And in doing that you might give

> them the ability to change...you just make them see it
> in a different light than they did. If there's any
> changing they have to do it themselves.
> *Foster carer, quoted in 'Testing the Limits of Foster Care'*

Your job as a foster carer is to help these children and young
people start to find different ways to behave. Your training, and
the support from your social worker, will help you to build the
necessary skills and knowledge. You will need to help the child
understand why they behave as they do – which is usually because
they have no other way of expressing the hurt, anger and
frustration inside them. You will need to help them think about
alternative ways to get those feelings across, and maybe plan some
strategies that they can use when things are difficult for them.
These can be as simple as showing a child how to count from ten
backwards when they think they are about to lose their temper.
Older children may need to develop more confidence and self-
respect, to help them stay away from friends who lead them into
activities like drug-taking or shoplifting.

## Education

You must make sure that the child is attending school, and you will
be expected to attend parents' evenings and other meetings
connected with the child's education. Wherever possible, children
will attend their usual school but, together with the child's social
worker, you may have to identify a new school and help the child
settle into this. You may need to develop close links with the class
teacher or designated teacher, who has responsibility for children
and young people in the school who are fostered. You will also be
expected to make sure that the child completes their homework.
Together with the child's social worker, teachers and education
specialists, you will need to make sure that the child gets help with
any problems they are experiencing. Some children may be
excluded from school and will have lessons with a home tutor or
attend a pupil referral unit, or the child you are caring for may have

learning or physical disabilities and attend a special school, that can meet their needs more fully than a mainstream school.

Many fostered children may have missed some schooling, or school may have been a low priority in their lives due to difficult situations they have been living in. As a foster carer, you will be expected to show them the value of education and take an interest in their schooling. You should read to and with the child (depending on their age), and have books available in your home (these could be from the local library).

> School had never been important to me, but my foster carer had this thing about education, and she really pushed me. She expected a lot from me and she made me want to achieve things – both for me and for her. And she'd go and speak to the school if she felt they weren't supporting me like they ought to. She was a total tiger, fighting for me like her cub!
> *Elinor, young woman who was fostered*

## Working with families

As a foster carer, part of your role will be to help the child maintain contact with their family. Parents and other relatives such as grandparents, cousins, aunts and uncles and close family friends may meet with the child in places like restaurants, parks or specialist contact centres. The children you care for may have contact with brothers and sisters who are in other foster care placements.

> You really don't know what to expect with some of these families and you have to keep an open mind. Some of the children's families are people you take to – you can see why they've got into difficulties – that life's been hard for them. . . Then there are some families who you just can't take to, you don't like them and you don't like what they've done to their child, but it's not

your job to make these judgements. What you have to do is keep an open mind and keep records – keeping evidence of the times they don't turn up or how upset the child was after their visit.

*Robyn, foster carer*

## Won't it be difficult to work with parents who have hurt or neglected their children?

Often when parents neglect their children it is because they have huge problems in their own lives, or they are affected by a mental health problem, or a drug or alcohol problem. Under pressure, a parent may find themselves taking out their anger and frustration on their child, or a mother who is suffering domestic abuse herself may be unable to protect her child from her abusive partner. Some parents may have had difficult and abusive childhoods themselves and can lack a basic understanding of what children need. Many parents do love their children but their lives have become so mixed up that they fail to care for or protect them properly.

As you meet parents of the children you care for, some of them may talk to you about their lives. This will help you to understand more about why a parent has neglected or hurt their child or allowed someone else to do so. Even if you find it hard not to judge a parent because of the way they have behaved, you will need to hide your feelings for the sake of the child, who probably still loves their parent very deeply. If you have worries about the way a parent or other relative treats the child, you should talk to your social worker or the child's social worker about this.

> Some parents are manipulative and you wonder why other people can't see that. You make a lot of progress with the child and you feel that going home isn't the right thing. You have a right to be heard and to have your views considered but ultimately it's not your decision. You have to hold on to what you achieved

with the child while they were with you, and hope that made a difference in the long run.
*Louise, foster carer*

## How will I learn to let go when a child leaves?

As a foster carer, unless you are a permanent carer for a child, your role is temporary – you are not there to replace the child's parents. But even so, it can be hard to say goodbye to a child or young person you have cared for. Experienced carers say that what helps them most is knowing that the child is happy to be going home to their parents, or that the child is going on to a new family who can provide permanence and stability. Sometimes children stay in touch with their foster carers after they leave – especially if they have lived with the family for a long time.

> Joanne was really keen on her freedom and I think that when she got to 16 and things didn't happen as she'd expected, she latched on to the idea that she could move out and go and live with her pals. She came back to us saying that she was grateful for everything we'd done for her but her social worker had found her a one-bed flat in an independent living scheme...When she moved, my professional hat said don't go and see her. My personal hat said I have to go!

> I still go and see Joanne about once a week and she's phoned me a couple of times. Sometimes when I knock at her door she doesn't answer, but I like her to know I'm still there for her. I tell her that our door is open if she needs us. She had a review meeting recently and her social work department hopes that she will stay in the area so our family can continue to offer her support. We are really all she has so I hope, one day, she will feel she can come to us for Sunday tea.
> *Foster carer*

# If I get upset about children leaving, will the fostering team think I'm bad at my job?

It is natural to have strong feelings for someone you have cared for, especially if this has been for quite a long period – and if you didn't have those feelings, you probably wouldn't make a very good foster carer. However, what is important is that you are able to manage those feelings and be supportive of the decisions that have been made for the child. Even if you don't think it is the best thing for the child to return to their family or be adopted by another family, you have to respect that decision, and not let the child know that you have concerns. But it's a good idea to make sure you have emotional support from someone close to you after the child leaves, as the loss may really hit once the child has left. Of course, everyone copes differently and some people will need more time to actively "grieve" the child's departure where others will cope by throwing themselves enthusiastically into new activities, like having fun with friends or planning a treat for themselves. However, you may already have other children in the house who will keep you fully occupied, so you may need to make sure you take some time out for yourself to acknowledge the sadness that you feel.

It is also fine to tell your supervising social worker that you feel upset by a child leaving and that you may need a bit of time before you take another child. Don't let anyone rush you into anything before you feel ready. All foster carers, even very experienced ones, get attached to children, although they may become more accustomed to children coming and going and get better at focusing on the positives, such as the child returning home. They also recognise that not every child will have the same effect on them. There will be some children where you will gently breathe a sigh of relief when they leave you, or some whom you will remember fondly even though you found their behaviour challenging when they were actually living with you.

Children need to know you will miss them – because everyone needs to feel wanted and valued, but you have to encourage the child to prepare and look forward to whatever is coming next in their lives. It's great if you can keep in touch, because it's helpful for children to realise that they can still hold people in mind even if you are no longer living with them. That helps them cope with the losses they already experienced with their birth family...Sadly, not all adoptive parents want that, but most do realise the value of this for the child.

*Yvonne, foster carer who prepares children for moves to adoptive families*

# 9

# Your role and responsibilities as a foster carer

Foster carers today have an important role and significant responsibilities. You will be expected to keep records and to attend meetings about the children and young people you foster. The introduction of Delegated Authority has also given greater freedom to carers to make more day-to-day decisions to ensure that the child or young person can enjoy similar opportunities to those of their peers.

As a foster carer, you have the right to expect that your views will be listened to, and that you will be treated as an important member of the team. This doesn't mean that you will always agree with the decisions that are made, but you should expect to feel that you have had an opportunity to express them and have them considered.

## Agreements and records

You will sign a "foster care agreement" when you are first approved by a fostering service, which will detail your role and responsibilities, and those of your service towards you. When a child is placed with you, you will sign a "placement agreement", to say that you have understood the work that the service is asking you to do with that particular child. You will be able to discuss with your supervising social worker anything that you don't understand or agree with.

Keeping records is an important part of being a foster carer, because you are in a situation to observe day-to-day changes in a child's life. It is important that you keep a separate book for each child. These records must, of course, be kept strictly confidential, and you will be required to hand them to the child's social worker when the child leaves your care.

The type of information you will be asked to keep should be as evidence-based as possible, focusing on, for example, any improvements the child makes, any changes in their behaviour or mood, accidents or injuries, and any contact the child has with their family. You will be asked to record dates of meetings, information about any medical appointments and the child's school progress. You will also keep records of any contact with the police, or any damage or theft by the child. You will also need to record any time when the child is being cared for by someone other than yourself or when the child was away from your home on contact visits, school trips, etc. Keeping detailed records can also be helpful for you as a carer, because if any allegations are made by members of the child's family or by the child or young person, it is good if you have your own recorded version of what happened on a particular date or occasion.

The following website has information about how to keep records: www.writeenough.org.uk/. Fostering Network (see Useful Organisations) produces a booklet called *Record Keeping Information for Foster Carers.*

## Attending meetings and reviews

As a foster carer, you will be expected to attend and contribute to meetings and Child in Care Reviews. These usually include the child's social worker, other professionals – such as a teacher or child psychologist – and the child's parents. If the child or young person is old enough, they may also attend some of these meetings, or they will be helped to express their views beforehand. These meetings are used to put together a plan for the child's future, to monitor its progress and to discuss any major changes or developments that may come up in the child or young person's life.

> You often hear young people complaining that they don't feel included in decisions made about them. As a foster carer you have to be their advocate – make sure their views are heard, and their opinions are listened to. You can say what you think as well, and that you don't necessarily agree with them, but it's important they feel listened to.
> *Shelagh, foster carer*

## Attending court

There may be times when you will be asked to attend court to give evidence to help the court reach decisions about the child's future. Records you have kept during the child's stay with you may be used as evidence in this process and you may be asked to write a brief report. You might be asked to provide evidence about something positive, like the progress you have seen in a parent's ability to look after their child, or something less positive, perhaps about the way a child has been upset by contact with their birth family. You should be offered help and support to do this.

You might also be attending court to give support to a child or young person who is giving evidence against an abuser, or telling the judge their feelings about their future. In Scotland, you will be entitled to attend hearings about the young person in your care. You may also be in court to give support to a child or young person who is themselves facing a charge, for example, for shoplifting or joyriding.

## Supervision and foster carer reviews

You will have regular meetings with your supervising social worker, to ensure that you are meeting the needs of the children in your care, and to offer support and a framework to assess your performance as a carer and to develop your skills. Foster carers also have regular reviews, to check that you and your household remain suitable to care for foster children and that your terms of approval are still appropriate. These reviews are governed by fostering regulations.

## Ongoing professional development

Kids come to us with quite complex issues who have experienced all sorts of things. Having a kid live with you and treating them like your own is important – but you also have to fully understand child development – and know what's typical and not typical. My advice would be to take all the training you're offered and learn about psychology, social and emotional development, etc, etc. You could have a child who wipes poo round the bedroom or hits you, or refuses to talk and you have to keep in mind there's a reason – like neglect, sexual abuse, foetal alcohol syndrome, neonatal abstinence. All children are lovely in different ways...you need to understand what's behind their behaviours, they don't just choose to behave like that. You need to understand that.

*Tee Green, specialist foster carer*

The training you undergo when you are prepared as a foster carer is the beginning of an ongoing process of learning and development. It may also be the start of possible specialism in certain types of fostering. As a foster carer, you are required to show that you can work to a high standard of professionalism, fulfil requirements and relate the training you receive to the needs of children you are looking after.

The ways in which foster carers receive professional development are evolving and the information given here is just an example of some of the processes in place when this guide was published.

As a foster carer in England, under the Training, Support and Development Standards, you may be expected to complete a workbook within 12 months of being approved, to show that you have understood the requirements of the role. Your supervising social worker or training staff at your service will help you, so you can demonstrate that you understand the requirements of the Standards and show how you put this learning into practice as you care for children. Some services run dedicated sessions to help carers meet the Standards and you will find that the ongoing training you attend is often geared towards helping you understand how your learning relates to them.

In Wales, the Care Council's Induction Framework for Foster Care and Short Break Care provides a similar ongoing process. As it says in the information describing this process: 'It is important to recognise that you will not be expected to meet all the outcomes within the framework before you are approved as a foster carer; the learning associated with progress will take time because induction is a process, and the first step to proficiency'.

In Scotland, the Scottish Government is currently working to create a learning and development framework within legislation, for foster carers.

## Am I bound by confidentiality?

As a foster carer, you will be given personal information about children and their families. As part of your role, you will be expected to respect confidentiality and not share the child or family's personal information with anyone who does not have a legitimate professional "need to know".

> Being a foster carer is stressful and we need people we can go to for support but you have to tread a careful line about not disclosing identifying details about the child and their parents. So you find ways to let off steam with your best mate, telling them about how things make you feel without giving confidential stuff away about the child...Talking to other foster carers also helps because they know the sort of issues you are dealing with.
> *Nav, foster carer*

# 10

# If things get difficult

> Fostering is bound to have its ups and downs –
> it's about people, and when you put families and
> relationships and feelings into the mix it gets
> complicated. You just have to do the best you can,
> and ask for help and support when you need it.
> *Lisa, foster carer*

Fostering is about working with children and families who are often
in difficult and upsetting situations, where there are no easy
solutions, and where compromises often have to be made. There
will also be frustrations, disappointments and injustices that you will
experience as a foster carer, for example, a child's parents may
complain about you or a young person may betray the trust you
have placed in them. So if you are someone who needs everything
to run smoothly, doesn't like uncertainty, or is badly affected by
misunderstanding or criticism, then fostering may not be right for
you. As a foster carer, you will be expected to have a reasonable
degree of resilience, to be able to find positives in situations that are
potentially challenging and to help children and young people
develop some of these characteristic themselves.

## Will I get support if I'm finding things difficult with a child?

You will have regular and structured supervision with your supervising social worker to check how things are going with the child or young person you are fostering. They should be able to offer you advice, extra training or support if you feel you need help with managing particular aspects of a child's behaviour. Your service will also have an "out of hours" phone number you can call if you are having problems, and some have helplines just for foster carers.

You may also find it very helpful to talk to other foster carers who have had similar experiences, and it can be a good idea to join your local foster carer support group if your service has one. Sometimes newly approved foster carers are "paired" with a more experienced carer whom they can contact when they want to talk something through.

It's also important to have support from your family and friends. You won't be able to share detailed information with them about a child's background (because you must respect the child's and family's confidentiality), but you will be able to talk about general problems you are facing. You could also simply spend some time with them relaxing and doing something completely different.

> Never be afraid to ask if you're struggling – there's no shame in asking for help. It's better to ask for help than let it go wrong. You get carers, especially new carers, who think that their service will think they're not coping and will move the child. Or it'll be a blot in their copybook. Sometimes it feels easier to ask other foster carers 'cos they've been through the situation themselves and have advice about how they handled it.
> *Neal, foster carer*

## What happens if I really can't cope with a particular child?

All relationships are about how well human beings get on together, and it's inevitable that there are going to be some children who settle well in your home, and some who don't. You may find that this can be managed in a short-term foster placement, with appropriate support. But sometimes both you and the child or young person can see that this isn't going to work for them. Ending a placement is very serious and should be a last resort, but in such cases, it's best to be honest with your supervising social worker – for everyone's sake.

You might find that caring for children of a certain age group doesn't work for them because of clashes with your own children, so you and your supervising social worker might discuss whether it would be better for you to take older/younger children in future. There may be other issues outside your control that affect how well a child or young person settles into your family, such as the young person being too far away from important friends, or too close to people whom it's not helpful for them to have contact with.

> As a foster child, you're not just going into a family but a community. There was one community who turned against the foster kids and they were blamed for everything that went wrong in the neighbourhood. The placement itself was brilliant – the foster carers were brilliant – but it was the community that wasn't accepting. It wasn't even a very rich area but the community had very strong views. There were very outspoken people in the area – there was even a petition started...In situations like that you don't have a chance to make it work.
> *Levi, 23, care leaver working with young people in care*

## What if I don't want to foster any more?

If you've had a foster placement that has been particularly difficult for you and your family, you might need a break before another child comes to live with you. But many carers find that after a difficult placement, having the next child feels much easier, and helps to restore their confidence. However, if you decide that fostering really isn't right for you and your family, you need to tell your supervising social worker.

Some people foster for long periods and then decide that it's time for a break, because their circumstances have changed. Some experienced foster carers take a break from fostering but use their time to train and support other carers. If you decide to leave fostering you can always reapply in the future, when you feel the time might be right for you to consider it again.

## What happens if a child damages my home?

Foster carers do need to consider having insurance and in many fostering services this is a requirement. There are several specialist home insurers for foster carers that may be more suitable than high street providers; ask your fostering service about these.

## I've heard that sometimes children make false allegations of abuse against their foster carers. What happens then?

Sometimes children do make false allegations against their foster carers. It may be that the child is very upset about something that's happening in their lives and doesn't know how to express these feelings, or they may feel that no one is listening to them. They may have suffered sexual or physical abuse in the past and not know how to explain who has actually harmed them. This may lead to children claiming that a foster carer or someone in the carer's family has physically, sexually or emotionally abused them. Some children who make such false allegations later retract them, and regret that they have made them. But social workers have to take every allegation very seriously in case someone really has harmed the child or young person – as, on rare occasions, this will actually be the case.

In your preparation to foster, you will learn how to provide "safe care", which helps you and other members of your family to consider how best to minimise the likelihood of such allegations being made.

> In the past, people sometimes got a bit too hung up about safe care and it got to the stage where you were frightened to hug kids, and you heard about people who'd been advised not to bathe a child unless the child was wearing their bathing costume…Now there's been a bit of a shift and, whilst still being sensible and vigilant, we are getting more of a balance towards what is "normal" and gives the right messages to children. You don't want children getting hang-ups about their bodies or not being able to ask for a cuddle when they're upset.
> *Linda, foster carer*

However, if it should happen that an allegation is made against you by a child or young person, your service has to investigate the child's claims. Understandably this can be very upsetting, and foster care laws and guidance say that if a child makes an allegation against you or a family member, you must be treated with respect, kept properly informed about what is happening and be given access to an independent person who can give you support and advice.

## What happens if the child's parent makes a complaint about how I'm looking after their child?

Any complaints made by the child's parent/s or anyone else must be carefully considered, in case the child is being mistreated in any way, or their needs are not being met. However, the context and nature of the complaint, and the parent's relationship with the local authority during court proceedings, will be taken into account, as it is understandable that a parent who feels upset that their child is in care may be inclined to be unfairly critical.

## What if I have a complaint?

As a foster carer, you have a right to complain if the service you receive does not meet the required Standards, or if you are experiencing problems with your supervising social worker. You can also make a complaint on behalf of a child you are caring for if you have concerns about their treatment. Your fostering service will advise you of their complaints procedure. However, it is always best to consider other ways of sorting out difficulties at an earlier stage, if possible, and you should talk to your social worker about this.

# 11

# Children's feelings about being in foster care

Being genuine has got to be the most important bit – someone doing it for the right reasons and they treat you with the same respect and dignity as they would their own children. Money doesn't come into the equation for them – they're not doing it for the money. From the outset, they need to make it known that you are part of the family unit. They need to be loyal and dedicated. You will stay with that child until the end and not just pass them off because they become challenging. You will support them with whatever issues they have.

*Matt, adult care leaver, working as an adviser to local authorities*

Imagine how you'd feel if you had got up one morning in your own home, with your own possessions and your own family around you, but by the evening you were going to bed in a totally different place, with strangers around you, and not knowing when you'd see your family again. It's hard enough to cope with this situation as an adult, but imagine how difficult this is for a child.

## How do children feel about coming into foster care?

Many children will be confused and scared. Others may be angry, withdrawn or just very sad and tearful. You may find that some children and young people who have been in foster care before may seem to take it in their stride, showing few emotions. You may also come across children or young people who are relieved to be away from a difficult situation at home. Every child is different and it's impossible to predict how a change of circumstances will affect them. However, you can be sure that many children will miss their own families a great deal and some will be keen to return home as soon as possible, however much they enjoy living with you.

> My carers were kind people and they had a nice house, but I was fretting all the time about my mum. Who was stopping her from going on her binges? I needed to know that everything at home was OK, and that made it difficult for me to settle.
> *Tiffany, 17, who was fostered as young teenager*

## What if their families have mistreated them?

Most children continue to love their families, no matter what has happened. They may not like the way someone in the family has behaved towards them, and they may be frightened of a particular person who has been living in the household, but overall they will continue to feel a strong bond to their family. Preparation for fostering will help you to think more about the feelings of children and young people towards their families, by asking you to think about the importance of relationships in your own life.

## What benefits do children get from fostering?

As a foster carer, you can play an important role in helping a child regain confidence and hope for the future. You will also be able to offer the child a period of stability and support to make sense of things that have happened to them in the past, and to help them prepare for whatever the future holds. Sometimes you may feel that you haven't achieved very much with a child, but it's amazing how many young people who have left foster care speak about something relatively small their foster carers did or said that made a helpful impression on their lives.

Another very important role that foster carers have is to give encouragement and praise. Children with low self-confidence can really benefit from being with someone who praises them for small achievements, encourages them to make the best of their educational and other opportunities, and makes them feel worthwhile and valued. This sort of support can be vital in helping a young person to turn their life around.

> If you can't be with your own mum and dad, you want to be with people who take the time to understand you, listen to you, put up with you when you're behaving like a right pain. You might get fed up with them at the time, nagging you to do homework and the like, but then you look back and you wouldn't have got to college or whatever if they didn't believe in you and want you to do well.
> *Jack, young person who was fostered*

## Will children want to call us mum and dad?

Many children who are fostered will be going home to their family, or continue to have regular contact with them, so it could be confusing for the child if they start thinking about you as replacements for their parents. You will need to make sure the child understands that you know they have a mum and dad, that you don't want to replace them, but that you do want to do what a good mum or dad would do for them. You can discuss with them what they are going to call you – perhaps you will decide to use your first name, or to call you Auntie or Uncle. It may be that the child wants to call you Mum or Dad, and you will need to discuss with your supervising social worker how best to manage this, as every situation is different.

## If we're long-term foster carers, won't the child become part of our family?

If you become long-term carers for a child who really can't return home to their family, then the child will become a permanent member of your family. You'll get to know each other well and share many of the day-to-day things that families share with each other, as well as special things like holidays and family celebrations. But the child may continue to have contact with their parents, brothers and sisters, and other relatives, and may want to phone them and talk about them. It can help to think about how you would look after a friend's child if the friend died or was permanently unable to look after them. You would provide love and care and support for the child, but at the same time would want the child to know about their parents.

> Here I feel loved a lot. When I'm really cross I say I want to leave this family. But I don't.
> *Louise, aged 11, quoted in 'If you don't stick with me, who will?'*

## Will children I foster want to stay in touch or come back and see me?

Some children will want to stay in touch with you and your children, especially if they have lived with you for a long period and you have built up a good relationship with them. You might find that some young people continue to visit you when they are adults – bringing their own children to see you!

Others will only stay with you for a short time and you may not see or hear from them after they leave. This is why it is important for foster carers to put together a book of photos with details and mementos of things the child has done while they were with them, often as part of life story work, to help the child to make sense of things that have happened in their lives. This can help to prevent a young person growing up wondering about the name of the family with the black cat and the funny-shaped garden, or where the beach was that they loved – because you have put all that information together for them.

## Can we stay in touch through social media?

Social media is used increasingly by the general population and many families openly share their photos and memories on public forums such as Facebook, sometimes with little understanding of the privacy options available. As foster carers, you will need to be very aware of the potential dangers of using social media. However, there are also positives in social media – such as the support many young care leavers receive from each other, and from former foster carers, during difficult times.

# 12

# Getting practical: money and careers

There are kids who fit really well into your family and are easy to care for. Then there's the kids you want to like but you can't help but think, when is this kid leaving us? Still, you do your best for all of them 'cos that's what you're doing it for, and you want to do a good job every time.
*Russ, foster carer*

## Is fostering a job?

Traditionally, fostering was seen as something that wealthy people did and for which they did not need or expect any financial support. Today, with a more diverse fostering population, it's recognised that many foster carers need to receive an allowance in order to be able to foster – they have bills to pay like everyone else. Some foster carers see themselves primarily as substitute parent figures, but others see themselves as "professionals" who have a fostering career. This can be reflected in the type of fostering they do, the fostering service they work for, and the skills, experience and motivation they bring.

# Do foster carers get paid?

Everyone who fosters receives an allowance to cover the cost of
caring for a child or young person in their own home. This is meant
to cover basics like food, clothes and all other costs of caring for the
child, recognising that children in care can cost more to care for
than other children. Allowances are set at local level in England,
Wales and Northern Ireland and vary widely, but carers should
receive at least the national government recommended minimum
rates. Scotland does not currently have a recommended minimum
allowance, and agencies decide on levels of payment within
parameters set out by the Scottish Government, which has
committed to making national recommendations in the future.

## Fees

Fee payments can be made on top of allowances to recognise a
foster carers' time, skills and experience. While all foster carers
receive an allowance, there is no requirement for fee payments to
be made and they can vary widely across the UK and according to
the age and needs of a child. Usually fee-paid carers receive
payment only when they have a child in placement.

Payments and allowances should be separate and clearly identified
so that foster carers know which portion of their fostering income
should be spent on caring for the child in their care, and which is
for the job that they do. Foster carers receiving a fee must register
as self-employed.

Some independent services may "employ" foster carers with terms
and conditions that may include paying carers for holiday periods
when the foster carer has no child living with them.

Fostering Network's website has more detailed information and
advice for carers about this (see Useful Organisations).

# What about tax and benefits?

Foster carers pay tax, so you will need to register with HMRC – they have special tax arrangements for carers that recognise your role and expenses. If you are on a low income, you may still be able to claim a range of benefits when you are fostering, but this may depend on whether you receive a fee for fostering and how the fee is made up – some high-paying fees may take you above the threshold for benefits. If you are worried about this, you should ask about it when you first apply to foster. The Fostering Network's website has more information on this, and they also have a range of publications and a helpline to help carers better understand the finances of fostering (see Useful Organisations).

# Do foster carers get opportunities to develop their skills or gain qualifications?

As a foster carer, you will be expected to attend training to update your skills and help you respond to children whose needs may be more challenging, including essential training in areas like safeguarding and first aid. This training will also help to ensure that you meet the relevant standards for foster carers. If you are a couple, both of you will need to undertake ongoing training, although not necessarily on the same day. Some services will have online training packages you can do in your own home. Carers will have a development plan for the year ahead, detailing what training they will undertake and how. This will be discussed each year in your foster carer review.

> Getting the training in managing difficult behaviour was a big help. We had this lad who was – I don't know, up and down all the time. Like a pot boiler. After the training I had these new ideas, and more confidence, and some of them really worked for him.
> *Barry, foster carer*

# 13

# The law, regulations and requirements

## Overview of the law

The way that all fostering services operate is governed by law, guidance and regulations. This chapter gives you some context of legislation that may affect you as a foster carer, but also the children and young people you would be caring for. This includes the legislation that governs children in care but also legislation that is designed to promote the wellbeing of young people leaving care.

## The law and looked after children

The legal term for a child or young person under the age of 18 who is in the care of the local authority is "looked after".

There are different ways in which a child may become looked after. Sometimes the parent asks for the child to be looked after; sometimes a young person approaches social services themselves; or sometimes a child or young person is removed from the family because there are concerns about their welfare.

In England and Wales, some children needing foster placements may be looked after by the local authority under a court order made under the Children Act 1989. This may be on a temporary order, but if a child is to remain in care for a long period the court may grant a care order, which lasts until the child is 18 (unless it's ended earlier by a court). Having a court order means that the local authority is able to exercise some of the "parental responsibility" that normally belongs to a family – in other words, it can make certain decisions about the child's welfare, even if the parents are not in agreement. But wherever possible, the local authority will try and work with the parents to obtain their agreement.

In Scotland, Children's Hearings make supervision requirements/ compulsory supervision orders for children, and some of these place children with foster carers. In an emergency, a Children's Hearing or Sheriff can make a child protection order or other short-term order. Other children are placed with foster carers when they are subject to permanence orders.

> I realised quite quickly that I needed to understand about the order the social worker had got for Suzi, when her parents just turned up on my doorstep.
> *Jenny, foster carer*

---

## COURT ORDERS

A court may grant a variety of temporary, long-term or even permanent orders to safeguard the welfare of a child. For example, in England and Wales there are emergency protection orders and interim care orders designed to be used for a few days or weeks while the child's and family's needs are assessed, and there are care orders that are made when plans for a child's future have been carefully considered, and which may last until a child is aged 18. In Scotland, the court can make a parental responsibility order to the local authority that gives the authority parental rights regarding all decisions about a child except adoption.

---

## What if the parent agrees to the child being fostered?

If parents are finding it very hard to care for their child or, for example, they need to go into hospital and have no one else to look after the child, they can ask the local authority to look after their child. This voluntary arrangement is often referred to as "accommodation". Parents can take their child home whenever they wish – although wherever possible, it's good to plan for a child to return home. In Scotland, a parent has to give 14 days' notice of their intention to do this, if the child has been accommodated for more than six months.

## How does the law affect young people leaving care?

In England, recent guidance and regulations mean that local authorities have a duty to support young people to remain with their foster carers after the age of 18, and up to the age of 25, if the young person and foster carer want this. This is known as Staying Put.

In Wales, the Welsh Government introduced the When I'm Ready scheme in 2015, to support care leavers who want to continue living with their foster carers after the age of 18.

In Scotland, Staying Put guidance encourages opportunities for young people to remain with their foster carers beyond the age of 18, but at the time of publication the duties of local authorities were still under review.

## The law and fostering placements

Under fostering legislation, local authorities must comply with certain duties when they place a child with foster carers; these duties are set out in Guidance and Regulations. They cover things like the suitability of a foster placement; record keeping; visits to children in foster care; the requirements for foster carers looking after children; and things such as meetings, children's contact with families and how plans are made for children's futures. They cover the rights of children and their families, and foster carers, to have access to representation and complaints procedures, if things go wrong.

## What about Care Standards?

There are National Minimum Standards for fostering services in England and in Wales, and National Care Standards in Scotland. These are standards that fostering services must meet when they provide a service. Together with the relevant fostering regulations for each country, they cover the standards of care, support and opportunities for education and personal development that must be provided for children; the responsibilities of foster carers; and the responsibilities that fostering services have for providing the service, and towards the foster carers they recruit and with whom they place children.

# 14

# What happens when children can't go home?

> We felt guilty at first about having these children as their mother seemed a really nice woman. And she was a lovely person in many ways, but her life was such a mess. She just couldn't give her children what they needed, she just had too many needs of her own, too many reasons why she couldn't provide the things they needed – security, consistency, basics like regular meals and clean clothes, and somewhere warm to sleep. She loved them but she couldn't put their needs before her own, which is something you have to do as a parent. It was like she'd never really grown up.
> *Tanya, foster carer*

## Why do some children go back to their parents and others don't?

Foster care is often used as a way of giving parents a chance to sort out their problems, so that they can take better care of their children in future. If the family is able to do this, and can show that they can care more appropriately for the child in future, the child will return home. But some families aren't able to make the adjustments to their lives that are needed to care for a child properly – even if they continue to love that child. Some children simply cannot return to their own parents because there is no home for them to go to, for example, unaccompanied refugee or asylum-seeking children. There may also be children whose parents have a serious or terminal illness, an ongoing mental health problem, or a severe learning disability, so the child cannot be cared for at home.

> You always hope that maybe your parents will turn their life around – but some people just can't change. Whenever you see them they're always trying to justify themselves, wanting to whitewash away what happened in the past, but you don't forget the things they did to you when you were a kid.
> *Carlotta, care leaver, 20*

## What happens when a child can't go home?

Even if children can't return to their parents, it may be possible for them to be cared for by someone else in the family or by someone who is a close family friend. If this is not possible, then a family must be found who can provide "permanency" and a sense of security for the child.

There are several different ways of providing permanency. It may be provided by long-term foster carers who care for a child well into adulthood, depending on the wishes and needs of the young person. It may be decided that the child will be adopted, if this is going to be in their best interests. Children and young people are always consulted and their wishes and feelings are carefully considered when any decisions are made about their future. Older children or those who continue to have a lot of contact with their family may prefer to be long-term fostered, whereas younger children or those with little or no family contact may benefit from being adopted.

Being part of the family taught me how society would
expect me to behave as an adult. Prior to living in the
family I believed that I could do what I wanted – there
was no way people were going to tell me what to do.
*Karen, quoted in 'Fostering Attachments'*

## Adoption

When a child is adopted, all responsibility for the child passes to
the new family, as though the child had been born into that
family. The local authority no longer has formal responsibility for
the child. Adoption is therefore a major event in a child's life, as it
may mean that a child loses family ties with important people like
grandparents and brothers and sisters – so it's only used where the
need to provide safety and emotional security outweighs the
benefits of a child remaining part of their own family. However,
many adopted children still have contact with their birth relatives –
even if they are now legally members of a new family.

## Will I be told if the child I'm caring for can't go home?

Plans for the child's future will be explained to you when the child
comes to stay with you, and you will be informed if the original
plans change or develop. As a foster carer, you should be
consulted and included in meetings about the child's future, so
you will usually be aware of decisions that are being considered.
However, many decisions are ultimately made by the courts, so
there may be times when several different options are being
considered for a child.

Some carers are particularly asked to care for children for whom
plans for adoption are being made. If you do this type of
fostering, your role is to help the child prepare for this important
move in their life, working alongside the child's social worker. You

may be asked to help with things like creating a life story book and to introduce the idea of moving to a new family to the child. You will also be expected to meet with the family who will be adopting the child and to work to a phased plan of meetings between the child and their prospective adoptive family.

## What happens if I don't agree that these decisions are in the child's best interest?

As a foster carer, there will be times when you are not in agreement with the decisions being made for the child, and this is something that experienced foster carers learn to manage. Your responsibility is to observe the child and keep records of anything that may affect the decisions made; your recommendations will be considered by the child's social worker and the court, but ultimately you will have to accept what has been decided. This may seem hard, but there may be issues that you cannot be told about for reasons of confidentiality and the court may feel that the child's long-term interests will be best served by the child returning home or to another family member. You may feel that as a foster carer you are able to provide "better" quality of care for the child, but the advantages of staying within their birth family and close to siblings and others to whom they have strong attachments may lead the court to decide that this care is "good enough". You have to bear in mind that this is not your child and that parents often really love their children and want to care for them, even if they have struggled in the past.

If you feel that you are not being properly involved in the process or listened to by the child's social worker, then you should speak with your supervising social worker.

> When Kyle came to us the plan was for him to be adopted, but then the couple who were interested pulled out. It left him really angry and confused. Now the plan seems to be that he will go home to his mum.

I know she wants to care for him, but he has complex
problems and she finds them hard to cope with. I'm
trying to do everything I can to help her prepare for
his return, because I know they both want this to work
out. I will give them all the support I can and I hope
and pray it turns out for the best.
*Grace, foster carer*

## What about my feelings of loss? How will I manage these?

Even the most experienced foster carers admit to feelings of loss
when a child they have cared for moves on, and if you didn't have
feelings of care and affection for the child, how would you be able
to provide them with a loving and secure environment? So you will
almost invariably experience very mixed feelings when a child
leaves you, even if you are fully in agreement with the plans that
have been made for the child's future. Carers may find ways of
coping with these feelings by talking about them, keeping busy,
taking a break, focusing on another child, or simply remembering
that they have given the child positive experiences while they were
in their care.

The day a baby or child leaves is a very sad time. It's
something you never get used to. It is painful, a bit
like the build-up to a funeral, but you can't let any of
your feelings filter through to the child. If they're old
enough you can prepare them for the experience, but
with younger ones you just carry on living and caring
for them and hope the good attachment you've built
up will help them attach to their new carers. If the
child is going to a good place it does help, and you
sometimes have the joy of the adopters to balance
your feelings. But we've had one child go to relatives
living in a really bleak house and that didn't feel so
good. You have to be guided by professionals and

accept the decisions they make. You're managing a whole whirlwind of feelings, but you remind yourself that you've done it before and you'll manage it again. *Julie and Jason, quoted in 'If you don't stick with me, who will?'*

## What if I want to adopt a child I'm fostering?

It's important not to think of fostering as a "short cut" to adoption, and most foster care is short-term, with different motivations behind it to those behind adoption. However, there may be some children who fit particularly well into your family, and you may be able to offer this child a level of care that they may not be able to receive elsewhere. For example, you may have learnt a great deal about a child's complex disabilities or emotional needs, and feel that you are prepared to offer lifetime care as part of your family.

If you decide that you want to adopt a child that you are fostering, you will need to apply to be assessed as a possible adopter.

> We went into the arrangement as long-term foster carers because we knew the girls had their own families, and we respected that. However, Natalie, the youngest girl, had this real thing about wanting to be adopted so she could feel she was really part of our family. The girls' social worker felt that it was going to be something that would benefit her so we started working towards this. Natalie was thrilled when the judge granted the adoption order. It seems to have given her more stability, which was the important thing for all of us
> *Foster carers who adopted*

# 15

# The rewards of fostering

You can't pretend it's easy but it's also one of the most
rewarding things you can ever do. If you really like
being around kids and you want to make a difference –
even in a small way – then I'd say find out about
fostering and see whether it's right for you.
*Neal, foster carer*

## Fostering sounds like hard work – so why do so many people do it?

People choose to foster for many reasons. Some carers say it's
something they've wanted to do for as long as they can remember,
but others find out about it later in life. Some people don't think
about becoming foster carers until their own children or
grandchildren grow up and they realise that they miss having
children in their homes. Some people start to foster because their
friends or family did it or they heard about it through a television or
radio programme, and felt they had something special to offer.

But whatever encourages you to consider fostering in the first

place, what is clear is that you really have to like children and enjoy
spending time in their company. People who've fostered for a long
time admit that there are some children they find easier than
others, and some children aren't always easy to like, but they enjoy
the satisfaction of knowing that they've made an important
contribution to helping a child who is going through a very difficult
time in their life.

> I think I tested her to the limits many times – how
> she kept me living there I will never know. She's a
> remarkable woman and I'd never have got where I
> am today without her encouraging me, every step of
> the way.
> *Adrianne, young adult who was fostered*

## What motivates foster carers?

Again, everyone is different. But really committed foster carers tend
to have one thing in common – they want to get the very best for
the children and young people they're looking after. The core part
of their role is providing a supportive, safe and caring environment,
but committed foster carers also want to make sure that everyone
else is playing their part in helping the child to get the assistance
and opportunities they deserve! They'll be working closely with the
school to make sure the child is receiving the extra support they
need in the classroom or playground; they'll be looking for ways to
develop the child's confidence and encouraging them to try new
hobbies and activities that boost their enjoyment and increase self-
esteem; and they'll be working with social workers and health
professionals to make sure the child is going to the physiotherapy or
therapeutic sessions they need.

Carers who can see things from a child's point of view are also the
ones who understand why it's important for a child to have contact
with their family. These carers recognise that children usually love
their parents – even if those parents have hurt them or let them

down in the past. These carers accept that many children will eventually return home, so will do everything they can to maintain strong links between children and their families. They may shed tears after a child leaves, but they'll genuinely be wishing their family all the best for the future. And if a child can't go home, these carers will help children to remember the happy times they had with their family, as well as making sense of the sad and more painful times.

> The satisfaction is in the small things. Some kids may never pass any exams but they get a swimming certificate and you're so dead proud of them and all choked up.
> *Brenda, foster carer*

## What do children and young people value most from foster carers?

Young people who have been in foster care say they want carers who make time for them, listen to them and stick with them through difficult patches in their lives. They want carers who respect that they have their own family, and don't try to replace them, but who also make them feel welcome and part of their lives. They really like it when foster carers show that they believe in them and encourage them to do their best, and when they celebrate their successes and take pride in their achievements. This is important on whatever scale it may be, whether it's sitting down to eat a meal at the table for the first time, getting through a day without being sent out of the classroom, or getting good marks in an important exam.

Often, looking back over their experiences in foster care, it's the seemingly small things that are the most important, and have the biggest effect on young people. They recall some little piece of advice or some practical way their foster carer helped them during a difficult time – and years later that small thing has stuck in their mind as having made a very big difference, because it showed that someone cared enough to have their interests at heart.

> All foster carers have to invest in the children and make
> positive attachments, but there will be grieving when
> children move on. It is a tough job, but no foster carer
> needs praise and accolades, but when you get the first
> smile, or a teenager gives you a nod of approval, when
> you know you've been appreciated – that's all you need
> as a foster carer. We don't want pats on the back.
> People say we are amazing, but we are ordinary people
> doing an amazing job and we do it for the children. I
> met a young care leaver whose story had me in tears
> and my wife and I decided from that moment to see
> what we could do and 10 years later we are still
> fostering. I think most foster carers come into fostering
> for altruistic reasons as they have experience of children
> they want to help, they have met children in care.
> *Brian, foster carer*

# References

Bond H (ed) (2005) *'If you don't stick with me, who will?' The challenges and rewards of foster care*, London: BAAF

Fostering Network (2013) *Why Foster Carers Care: How understanding values can transform relationships and improve services*, London: Fostering Network, available at: www.thefostering network.org.uk/sites/www.fostering.net/files/uploads/pdf/why-foster-carers-care-report-v5.pdf

Jayne H (2010) *Dale's Tale*, London: BAAF

Schofield G (2003) *Part of the Family: Pathways through foster care*, London: BAAF

Sinclair I (2005) *Fostering Now: Messages from research*, London: Jessica Kingsley Publishers

Sturge-Moore L (ed) (2005) *Could you be my Parent? Adoption and fostering stories*, London: BAAF

Wade J, Sirriyeh A, Kohli R and Simmonds J (2012) *Fostering Unaccompanied Asylum-Seeking Young People: Creating a family life across a 'world of difference*, London: BAAF

Walker M, Hill M and Triseliotis J (2002) *Testing the Limits of Foster Care: Fostering as an alternative to secure accommodation*, London: BAAF

Warman A (2007) *Who am I and What do I do?*, London: BAAF

Warman A (2009) *Recipes for Fostering*, London: BAAF

Youell B (2016) *Parenting a Child Affected by Sexual Abuse*, London: BAAF

# Useful organisations

**Fostering Network**

**Head Office**
87 Blackfriars Road
London SE1 8HA
Tel: 020 7401 9582
www.thefosteringnetwork.org.uk

Unit 10, 40 Montgomery Road
Belfast BT6 9HL
Tel: 028 9070 5056

2nd Floor, Ingram House
227 Ingram Street
Glasgow G1 1DA
Tel: 0141 204 1400

1 Caspian Point
Pierhead Street
Cardiff Bay CF10 4DQ
Tel: 0800 316 7664

Works to help ensure that all children in foster care enjoy the best life chances. Provides advice, training and resources for foster carers and those working with children in care, and publishes *Foster Care* magazine. The Fostering Network also runs general and legal advice helplines.

### FosterTalk

Provides professional support services to foster carers UK-wide, with a specialised range of support including legal, financial and emotional issues.
Tel: 01527 836 910
www.fostertalk.org

### Fosterline

A free, confidential helpline for foster carers and those thinking of becoming foster carers. Run by FosterTalk (on behalf of the Department for Education).
Fosterline: 0800 040 7675
www.fosterline.info

### CoramBAAF

A membership organisation for all those working with or caring for children who are in care or adopted. Provides advice, training and a wide range of publications on adoption, fostering and child development.
41 Brunswick Square
London WC1N 1AZ
Tel: 020 7520 0300
www.corambaaf.org.uk

# Useful reading

The books listed below are available from CoramBAAF. Please visit www.corambaaf.org.uk or contact 020 7520 7517 for more details.

## BOOKS FOR ADULTS

### Parenting

Kate and Brian Cairns, *Attachment, Trauma and Resilience*, 2016
Draws on Kate and Brian's personal experiences with three birth children and 12 fostered children to describe family life with children who have experienced attachment difficulties, loss and trauma, and suggests what can be done to promote recovery and develop resilience.

Vera Fahlberg, *A Child's Journey through Placement*, 1995
Invaluable for all those involved in childcare, this book contains the theoretical knowledge base and skills necessary for understanding and working with children who are separated from their families. Comprehensive sections on attachment, separation and child development are included, all illustrated with case studies.

Clare Pallett *et al, Managing Difficult Behaviour*, 2015
This handbook, aimed at foster carers, teaches techniques in how to
manage difficult behaviour in fostered children and improve
relationships. The practical tips, exercises and case examples help
you to learn in your own way, and in your own home.

Gillian Schofield and Mary Beek, *Promoting Attachment and
Resilience*, 2014
This practical guide is designed to support foster carers and adopters
in offering the best possible sensitive care for troubled children who
have often experienced trauma and loss. Secure Base is a model of
caregiving that is based on theories of attachment and resilience
while also drawing on placement research. The guide is
accompanied by a DVD.

## Useful guides

Kate Cairns and Chris Stanway, *Learn the Child*, 2004
A resource pack (containing a book and CD-ROM with a Powerpoint
presentation) which looks at how foster carers, teachers and social
workers can help looked after children to gain full benefit from their
lives at school.

Robbie Gilligan, *Promoting Resilience*, 2009
This pioneering book applies the concept of resilience to work with
children in residential and foster care. Packed with practical ideas on
how to improve the quality of life for children in care using
relationship networks in their family, school and leisure activities.

Tony Ryan and Rodger Walker, *Life Story Work*, 2016
This popular and practical guide is essential reading for anyone
involved in life story work with children. Accessibly presented and
attractively illustrated.

## Parenting Matters series

This series of books looks at a number of health needs and

conditions that are often associated with looked after children. Authoritative information about the condition and how it affects children is followed by personal stories from adopters or carers that describe day-to-day life with an affected child. The series covers a range of conditions, including mental health issues, developmental delay, autism spectrum disorder, emotional and behavioural difficulties, parental substance misuse, domestic violence and sexual abuse.

## BOOKS FOR CHILDREN

Hedi Argent and Mary Lane, *What Happens in Court?* 2003
A user-friendly guide to help children understand the role a court might have in their lives. Easily understandable and brightly illustrated.

Michelle Bell, *Elfa and the Box of Memories*, 2008
A beautifully illustrated picture book for young children on the importance of memories, sharing them, and finding ways of keeping them alive. Suitable for children aged 4–10.

Jean Camis, *My Life and Me*, 2001
This colourful and comprehensive life story book will help children living apart from their families develop and record memories of their past. Written by a social worker with extensive experience of direct work with children, *My Life and Me* is supplied with practice guidelines.

Jean Camis, *We are Fostering*, 2003
Designed along similar lines to *My Life and Me*, this colourful and durable workbook will help birth children to know their history and role in the family, and prepare them to welcome foster brothers and sisters into their homes and lives.

Angela Lidster, *Chester and Daisy Move on*, 1999
This popular and engaging picture book is for use with children

aged 4–10 who are moving on to adoption, to help them explore feelings about their past and their moves, and to help carers identify these issues from the child's perspective.

Paul Sambrooks, *Dennis Duckling* series
In this series of books, Dennis Duckling and his sister Donna have to leave their family as they can no longer look after them. They go to live on a new pond where they begin to make new friends and are cared for by grown-up ducks. The series covers issues including who makes the decisions about where the ducklings will live, and several alternative endings to their story, including going to live with relatives, or returning home. Suitable for use with children aged 4–8.

Jill Seeney, *Morris and the Bundle of Worries*, 2008
In this charming picture book, Morris the mole has a big bundle of worries, but learns that talking about problems, and facing worries with the help of others, is more helpful than hiding fears. Suitable for use with children aged 5–10.

Shaila Shah, *Fostering: What it is and what it means*, 2016
This is a short, brightly illustrated guide to fostering for children and young people, covering the different types of fostering, how children come to be fostered, parents, contact and many other questions. Designed to be worked through with a child before and during foster care.

# Find out more about fostering with **Capstone**

We have local teams across England to support you with your fostering enquiry. Whether you are simply looking for more information or want to discuss how to become a foster carer, we can give you free, friendly advice.

We currently support over 600 foster carers from 16 local offices and offer a range of training and 24/7 support in each local area. It's important to us to offer a range of activities and get-togethers for our fostering families. If you'd like to join our next event in your local area please get in touch or visit our website to find out more.

Building brighter futures

# Excel
# Fostering

*making tomorrow a brighter day for children*

## Could you foster a child?

## 1000's of children in the UK urgently need foster homes NOW

# 01253 712734

## www.excelfostering.com

**243/245 Clifton Drive South, St Annes, Lancashire FY8 1HW**

# What does a foster carer look like?

They look just like you!

Children and young people need someone to care and love them regardless of that persons gender, marital status, age, race, religion, sexuality, qualifications or financial status.

Take Fosterline's quiz to see if you could foster and change lives.

**www.fdb.ac/fosterline**

If you would like to find out more about becoming a foster carer call Fosterline for free confidential advice on **0800 040 7675.** Advisers are available Monday to Friday 9.00am to 5.00pm or visit **www.fosterline.info** to find out more.

**Fosterline**
**0800 040 7675**
your fostering advice service

**www.fosterline.info**

Department
for Education

"FosterTalk"
supporting those who care

Fosterline is funded by the Department for Education and delivered by FosterTalk.

# Children Need You

## Make a difference - become a foster carer

**Futures for Children are looking for foster carers in:**

*The North East, West & East Midlands, East Anglia, London and the South*

**Contact us and make a difference!**

**Call us on 0800 195 3644 to find out more!**

 **www.futures-for-children.org**

 **www.facebook.com/futures-for-children**

**keys** FOSTERING

- *Keys Fostering is looking to Foster carers who can provide a loving and caring home for looked after children.*

- *Keys Fostering is an independent Fostering Agency based in Newport, South Wales.*

- *Keys Fostering is part of Keys Group, a large specialist childcare company that provides residential childcare and education to looked after children.*

- *As a Keys Foster carer you will receive generous weekly payments for each child you care for as well as additional payments to cover holidays for the child, birthdays and Christmas presents.*

- *You will receive pre and post approval training, 24 hour support and 2 weeks paid holidays.*

- *T: 0800 043 4329*
  *E: enquiries@keysfostering.co.uk for an application pack or more information*
  *W: www.keysfostering.co.uk*
  *A: 24 Bridge St, Newport, NP20 4SF*

# www.fostering.com